Notebooks of a Dilettante

NOTEBOOKS OF

Leopold Tyrmand

A DILETTANTE

❦   ❦   ❦   ❦

THE MACMILLAN COMPANY

"American Diary," "From the Notebook of a Dilettante," "A European from America in Europe," "On Revolution and Related Matters," and "On Permissiveness and Correctitude" originally appeared in *The New Yorker*.

THE MACMILLAN COMPANY
866 Third Avenue, New York, N.Y. 10022
Collier-Macmillan Canada Ltd., Toronto, Ontario

Library of Congress Catalog Card Number: 76-96748

FIRST PRINTING

Printed in the United States of America

CONTENTS

*I admit to having a perfect horror
of a dictatorship of theorists.*
ORWELL

*To see what is in front of one's
nose needs a constant struggle.*
ORWELL

Notebooks of a Dilettante

1.

American Diary

JANUARY 20, 1966

America reached by sea. This situation is, in a sense, similar to that of Christopher Columbus, and one should not penetrate America too far or too deeply but imitate the celebrated discoverer. A slight touch on the edge gives the best results. If one stays only on the fringe, people will remember one and give one's name to universities.

NEW YORK

The first day. An ad of Eddie Condon playing in the neighborhood restaurant. All seems larger and better here than in Europe with the exception of frankfurters, which are not as good as in Frankfurt.

Down to Washington, D.C., by car. I am terribly occupied with adjusting my sense of distance. The vastness of this continent makes me think with excessive sympathy of the nice, cosy, secure claustrophobia of Europe.

WASHINGTON, D.C.

Here in this huge city, I am more than ever frightened of the world, called "wide" by common folk and optimistic philosophers. More intelligent people know it is just round.

But my problem is how to find myself in an absolutely new notion of dimension. The hugeness swallows a human being. Nothing can be reached with God-given members only; it is necessary to get something more from Ford or General Motors. But how many and what kind of members can we get from even the most powerful industry in the world? Such prospects are rather limited, thank God.

In the afternoon, a ride to Accokeek, Maryland. The name and landscape are well known from the tales of Fenimore Cooper. "Read the classics, boy," one of my uncles used to repeat. It's good that America already has some classics. One feels immediately at home with a classic.

❧ *A large proportion* of Washington's policemen are Negroes. They patrol the streets and watch federal buildings and most neural centers of administration; Negro policemen regulate the traffic and issue passes to important executive offices and places of political significance. Of course, they are well-armed—pistols, clubs, and other symbols of a policeman's authority and strength hang loosely at their sides.

It's these simple but completely overlooked facts that amaze a European. I said to an American friend: "Look, but he is armed . . . ," pointing to a Negro policeman. "Obviously, a policeman is armed," he answered. It's not so obvious to a European, considering that the policeman belongs to an ethnic minority group that thinks itself persecuted, oppressed, or at the least deprived of equal rights. Europeans, too, have for centuries had minority problems, yet no one ever saw a Ukrainian or a Jewish policeman in pre-war Poland, nor can one see today an Italian policeman in French Savoie, an Austrian policeman in Italian Tirolo, or a Hungarian policeman in Romanian Banat. There are certain mistakes Europeans never commit. A minority group gets arms only when it is no longer a minority and when feelings of persecution and injustice—so dangerous in moments of anger and revolt—are beyond any doubt rooted out.

I never read in the Communist press that there were Negro policemen in America. Maybe I don't really know anything about the Negro problem here?

❧ *It takes but a glance* to notice that tomatoes and billiard tables, highways and the lust for life, are unquestionably larger here than in Europe. But the consequences are not always obvious, either to Americans or to us. We, for example, tend to overlook what great literature, great idealism, and great determination are derived from this scale of distance and streets. Americans sometimes seem to forget what grave responsibility towards the world weighs upon them and what great skill is necessary to fulfill great obligations.

❧ *The roads* are cleaned up and neat, but the pavements are full of ice and snow. I nearly break my ankles with every step. On the road, there are many cars, but on the pavement, only me. I alone try Connecticut Avenue by foot.

❧ *A huge ad* on the back of a bus shows a gentleman looking with concern at his watch: "What do you do when your chauffeur quits? Ride D.C. Transit. Comfortable—Convenient—Economical."

❧ *Mr. S.* from the Experiment in International Living wants me to speak on TV—an interview. I wonder what I could say on an "Educational Program?" EIL is an organization devoted to YMCA–Boy Scout ideals, and Mr. S. himself does not seem to be well-informed about my books, my involvement in jazz, or the political intricacies of Eastern Europe. He is a nice, quiet, middle-aged New Englander who does not react too enthusiastically to my hopeless stabs at brilliance. But I agreed to an interview in two days.

❧ "*We Americans* are simple." someone said to me.

"It is a very noble virtue in the contemporary world which sickens us with its complexity," I answered a bit too hastily. "Your pragmatism considers simplicity an advantage, not a drawback; that if something can be simplified—it works better . . ."

I realized my enthusiasm for American simplicity did not please my companion. "But . . .," I floundered, "you tend toward every kind of simplification. When you look at life in Communist countries, you see societies either as full-blooded Communist societies or as fully enslaved by the Communists. But reality is more complex, and afterwards you wonder why you did not understand what was going on . . ."

At this point I felt he had lost interest in our conversation. His reply was merely polite.

❧ *In the morning* on the bus, a girl sat next to me, pulled a book from her bag and started to read: *The Three Ways of Philosophical Thought in Ancient China.*

❧ *The TV interview*—what a surprise! Mr. S. metamorphosed himself from a somnolent boy scout into a whimsical "causeur" whose perverse remarks make every answer easy, a man of sophisticated opinions on jazz, political conformity, and striptease. The interview wings its way. There's something terribly American in the transformation of Mr. S.

❧ *No complaints* about the snowy blizzard from Washingtonians; they are up a mark in their perennial competition with New York. New York recently had an electric power blackout and a crippling transportation strike, plunging Washington into a deep inferiority complex. With the biggest snow storm of the century, Washington regains its feet.

❧ *How to lose* one's ambition and remain creative? Life in this country gives an answer at each step. The abundance of everything is so overwhelming that ambition seems a waste of time. Every dimension is possible and attainable without having to inform every last news reader. "What is this superb palace? To whom does it belong?" I ask a passer-by. "I don't know," he answers. "It must be private property. Ask the janitor." When I watched Hollywood movies as a child in Warsaw, I always wondered why no one (except the local paper and police) knew about *such* a murder, in *such* an estate, committed on *such* a millionaire. Now I understand.

❧ *Americans are* killingly exact, especially where a man's name and profession are concerned. They don't enjoy the gradual discovery of another person. They ask straight out: "What is your name, please?"
"Tyrmand."
"Would you be so kind as to spell it?"
I'm spelling it.
"How do you pronounce it?"
I'm pronouncing it. And so on, the whole evening long.
In Europe when a name is indistinct, we do not insist. We assume that if someone does not make his name clear,

he must have a reason. After all, we can always ask the host if it is really important. But here in America, the name has some mystic appeal. An amazing number of novels, plays, and movies have plots built on the fascinating intrigue involved in the changing of a name. "What is your name?" asks the morally upright hero, having the murderer at gunpoint. "Wardsworth Coullogh," answers the villian with trembling lips. "You liar!" shouts the hero triumphantly, "your name is Moriarty McClapham!"—and kills him. Everyone nods approvingly, on the screen and in the audience, for what a sin and incredible abjectness it is to change one's name! It's astonishing how strong the aristocratic mythos of a name is in this democratic society.

"You are a writer, aren't you?"

"Oh, you might say so . . . ."

"Well, are you, or aren't you?"

"In a sense."

It's always most embarrassing to explain that in Europe writing is considered more a vocation than a profession: if someone is too sure he is a writer, we have some doubt as to whether he really is. The art of conversation without the burden of exactitude is little known; Americans ignore the pleasure of remarks which are of little concern to anyone. I had to elaborate a method of defense.

"What do you like best in America?"

"America . . ."

The odd inaccuracy of that statement clearly impresses every collocutor. He or she smiles but does not withdraw.

"And what do you dislike most here?"

"America . . . ."

"I beg your pardon?"

"Let's make it more precise: too much of America."

He or she expresses a certain discomfort. He or she asks if I would like another drink and disappears into the crowd. I hear from a remote corner: "What a strange fellow . . . So difficult to talk to . . ." But in my opinion I was unquestionably accurate.

❧ *Columbus and* Amerigo Vespucci were probably the last who could afford to compare America to Europe. Now, five centuries later, every comparison is pure nonsense. America is America, and the European scale of standards is useless here. To hell with it!—as Hemingway would say.

❧ *Dinner in a* suburban home. Marvelous old Persian pottery, old Persian rugs, and old Persian miniatures. Diplomats, congressmen, lawyers. Open-minded, liberal, enlightened, democratic, antisegregationist, and wealthy. But not embittered. Bitterness always seemed to me a special privilege of every social elite, and lack of it a sign of superficiality. But I may be wrong; there is nothing more deceptive than superficiality. One guest entertained me with a long speech about elective monarchy in seventeenth-century Poland. He knew much more about it than I.

There are no monuments of Kościuszko and Pulaski in Warsaw, but there are in Washington. Fatherland of fatherlands? No, that would be too simple and too European a standard.

❧ *Washington's monuments*—one, especially, exemplifies a most significant defeat of the European scale of values. It's an unimpressive slab of stone, a memorial to one of the United States' greatest presidents. The words inscribed are:

In September 1941 Franklin Delano Roosevelt called his friend, Supreme Court Justice Frankfurter, to the White House and asked the Justice to remember the wish he then expressed:

"If any memorial is erected to me, I know exactly what I should like it to be. I should like it to consist of a block about the size of this (putting his hands on the desk) and placed in the center of that green plot in front of the Archives Building. I don't care what it is made of, whether limestone or granite or whatnot, but I want it plain, without any ornamentation, with the simple carving, 'in memory of——' "

A small group of living associates of the President, on April 12, 1965, the 20th anniversary of his death, fulfilled his wish by providing and dedicating this modest memorial.

The virtue of modesty is not as rare among great statesmen as many believe. Yet I can imagine the discussions and arguments arising should someone like to commemorate Gladstone, Bismarck, Clemenceau, or Lenin in the same way. He would be swept away in a storm of indignation. Evidence of one other facet of American simplicity—the greatness of simplicity itself.

NEW ORLEANS, LOUISIANA

To New Orleans by air. In a full bus on Tulane Avenue, a Negro girl would not sit next to me. I felt segregated for the first time since the Nazis left Poland. *"Le racisme à rebours?"* And who, in this case, was the victim? I, whose admiration for the New Orleans Negroes and their contribution to the culture of the twentieth century led me to write a book about them. But how could this girl know about it? All the rules of racial persecution and collective responsibility applied to me as well.

Vieux Carré on Friday evening. Beauty and genuineness are canned. Originality, stylishness, and the picturesque were given by history and nature, but the Americans could not check themselves from editing it, making it up. This city has a real treasure, something the rubbish guidebooks call "romantic" or "pictorial." Now it's been made false. The carefully prepared and preserved au-

thenticity of a unique, colorful tradition has been pack-
aged and wrapped like some delicious food.

❧ *Not all is* canned beauty in New Orleans. Last evening I took part in something truly touching, trueborn
and unstained: some sexagenarians played jazz in Preservation Hall on St. Peter Street. Sheer joy and sheer
serenity! Meet the Legend! Mr. Legend—George Lewis—
and others blow their clarinets and cornets with dignity
and wisdom. They produce simple and noble music, pure
in its intentions. If not always inventive and immaculate
in phrasing, it is always magical in its elemental artistry,
tenderness, and wit. I'm helpless when I want to describe
it; it is not possible to describe sincere, emotional experience. "Just a closer walk with thee . . ." brings tears to
everyone's eyes. Aged ladies in minks sit with effort on
the dirty floor as the band breaks into "Jada". . . .

❧ *Strange feeling* of familiarity! I wander around
North Rampart Street, admiring the warm beauty of daub
in the church of Notre Dame de Guadelupe, strolling
through Congo Square, Canal, and Basin Street, around
St. Louis Cemetery. I wrote a book about this city, never
having been here. Now I recognize well-known places
never seen. A burying ground and ruins of Storyville with
its memories of bygone pleasures lie side by side. Jazz—
in Europe a symbol of passion or of joy, of spiritual freedom or of cultural independence—is here like oxygen.
Like the Creole gumbo I ate with people from Preservation Hall, the real gourmets of this city's spell. Jazz and
gumbo alone are here superb, unique, and natural. Of
course, now the big stream of progressive creativity in
jazz is far, far away—replaced by bad, suspect painting,
dull galleries, and boring, second hand, artistic "boheme."
But what was done in the last eighty years will never

pour out of this town; the names of French Quarter, Bourbon Street, and Saint James Infirmary echo in the consciousness of our century. And, last, there are very few museums in the world where part of a brothel is proudly exhibited; a stone from the gate of Madame Lulu White's *maison de tolérance* decorates the New Orleans Jazz Museum and evokes nostalgia. If we note that Miss White's house was torn down but a few years ago, the importance and uniqueness of New Orleans in contemporary civilization strikes us forcefully.

❦ *Everyone smiles at you* in America; it is a social feature. Everyone, with the exception of the hotel service. They grin sometimes, but this grin makes people shiver.

❦ *Beyond any doubt*, New Orleans is the Food Capital of America. Many are prone to consider food of civilizational value. For me food belongs to culture. The overwhelming feeling of pride induced by swallowing something, the texture and fragrance of which triggers a chain of mental associations, is, despite other appearances, a cultural activity. New Orleans cuisine, whose history is long and intricate, succeeded in engendering *a style*, the importance of which transgresses all endemic denominations, like Creole cooking, or the Southern kitchen. Abundance of food is usually an effect of industriousness, but a great tradition in cooking is always the fruit of snobbery. I'm sure the latter is just that cultural ingredient of which New Orleans, from its beginnings through its heyday, was never short. As with every genuine cultural or artistic accomplishment, it suffers from a frustrating deficiency of recognition, for everything that emerges by means of snobbery as a cultural power is mystically doomed to suffer from snobbery as a caricatural power. How many torpid, insipid American snobs from coast to coast daily repeat that in order to eat well, one is forced to go to Europe, chiefly France. With their sterilized American inferiority complex, they are incapable of discovering an idea of culinary subtlety and sophistication within the boundaries of this country. But if someone should say: "Go to New Orleans," they'd answer: "I saw it in the movies," thus proving once more the contemporary disassociation of intelligence from experience that, of all things, may give lethal results in *gourmet* matters.

HOUSTON, TEXAS

The most exhausting feature here is the method of communication. Americans ignore our general principle for communicating important matters—the rule that not all is to be said. There are things, mainly wishes, that we do not express but rather make felt. To Americans one has to speak directly. Allusion, which constitutes the only possibility of accepting before being asked or without having to ask, is unknown. If you want to be invited to an American's home, you must tell him so—something that in Europe would be unthinkable.

❦ *Luncheon in the Hotel Rice* with the Houston Rotary Club. The largest section of International Rotary, as I'm informed. Splendid hall, some hundred people, choral singing, speeches—all around the specific accent of American heartiness and valiant joking. But, the lights go down slowly; the Star-Spangled Banner streams proudly—encouraged with unsophisticated efficiency by a silent fan—the audience sings the anthem. At once I have the impression of facing an organized, enormous strength. An almost military power emanates from these middle-class, suburban, downtown-minded executives, associates, managers, and assistant directors—a conscious, disciplined, social might, constructed differently from that in totalitarian regimes but probably the only kind that could successfully and forcefully resist any encroachment from right or left. I thought: "How fascinating to see middle-class executive directors looking dangerous and fierce while standing in rank! Even under Communism, a director looks miserable out of his office. . . ."

One of my table partners asked if there were Rotary Clubs in Poland. I answered no, as today Poland is ruled by Communists. He said: "Ah, I see." After a while he asked: "What then is the substitute for Rotary?" "Look . . . ," I started, but I took pity on his helpless devotion to the Rotarian cause and wanted to comfort him, so I said: "We had a Polish YMCA for a while after the war. But it was liquidated in 1949." His brow was marked by intense reflection. "And now," he asked pointedly, "what is the substitute for the YMCA? . . ."

I had to withdraw. How could one explain to a Texan why there are no substitutes for socially valuable elements in a Communist country?

❧ *On the University of Houston campus,* I saw a group of students in passionate discussion in the middle of the lawn. I approached. They were speaking about God. Under communism, even anti-Marxist students never discuss God (except theological faculties, of course). Not because it is forbidden but because they think it's a waste of time. God is not an immediate need for them; they need freedom, jazz, independent literature, and a pair of blue jeans.

❧ *In Houston* the past tense is out of use. The present tense is avoided, and everyone speaks only in the future tense. For example: "This steak is delicious," I try to flatter my host. "You'll have to come next year," he assures me. "You'll see what steaks we have in Texas. . . ."

In the Astrodome, the biggest covered living room in the world, the guide repeats: "In our space age . . ." One must admit that it applies here, much more than in Warsaw, Paris, or Boston.

I attended the theatre in Houston. What a surprise! I saw Pirandello's *Right You Are If You Think You Are*, presented by the Alley Theatre on an arena stage in such a delicate, inventive, and imaginative way, with such an exquisite balance of directing, acting, staging, and lighting that even the best London, Paris, and Warsaw companies might feel deep, corrosive envy.

🌿 *Manned Spacecraft Center in Seabrook.* What fascinated me was not the lunar landscape training grounds or the rockets and equipment. I do not grasp much of it; I am too engrossed in what I don't understand on this globe to get involved in nonunderstanding the cosmos. (When we drove through a suburban residential area—full of architectural canned beauty—my host pointed out to me a good-looking man who was in the midst of a bitter fight with a water hose. "That's McDivitt," said my host, "from the Gemini flight." I don't know how Mr. McDivitt performed in space, but I can confirm beyond any doubt that he had serious difficulties mastering the mystical, elemental force of a water hose.) We arrived at a private cocktail party: there were scientists (with wives), engineers (with wives), and wives (without astronauts). This was a real revelation. One may see a living Russian astronaut at press conferences or in parades, but no one sees the living wife of a Russian astronaut (except in the newsreel)—they are extremely well guarded because as women they are obviously more inclined to boast of their husbands' space exploits than the astronauts themselves. But I was most struck by the fact that all these physicists and specialists in rocketry and gravitation spoke to me about film, theatre, the latest books of Bellow and Capote, and were better oriented *vis-à-vis* Cardinal

Wyszynski's affairs than an average newspaperman in France. In Europe for years we have been discussing the intellectual limitations of scientists: they complain that they are barely able to follow all that concerns their own specialties, so how can they know about Kafka? But these Americans can. Every one of those wives is probably drowning in the maelstrom of bringing up six kids and is still damnably lettered. How do they manage? When do they get time?

SANTA FÉ, NEW MEXICO

In this best of civilizations, the hotels are true ulcers.

I sat on a bench in Santa Fé Plaza in front of the Old Spanish Palace of the Governors, where an elderly gentleman in a black Stetson asked me a question. When I answered in my underpolished English, he said: "You're from the North, aren't you? Illinois or Michigan, right?"

I was flattered, as any foreigner is who is taken for a native.

❧ *I don't like stylization* in architecture and art, but I have to admit that what has been done in Santa Fé makes sense. With time, it may create a new style or a new art. The role of the Indians in this creative process reminds one of the Negroes' role in jazz. The wonderful, rich, Indian sense of color, whose roots are genuine and imaginative rather than technological, brands all that is painted, carved, and woven here with the mark of fresh inspiration. The churches of San Miguel and El Cristo Rey are treasures of North American iconography. The symbiosis of primitive wood-painting and naive holy-figure-carving with modern techniques has already had a novel effect on architecture and handicraft. With time, this may become the cradle of enormously valuable invention.

❧ *I always believed* that Texans were terribly anti-Mexican. It is not true. Everyone, the dedicated Birchite included, repeated to me in Houston: "You should go to San Antonio. There you really feel Mexican. Mexican food, Mexican women, Mexican atmosphere. Not like here. . . ." I felt saturated with pro-Mexican snobbery: for a while I took pride in my own dark hair.

In Santa Fé, there's an analogous attitude toward the Indians. "His parents were real Pueblo Indians," a waspish lady said to me during a party, indicating a handsome young painter dressed in the best Greenwich Village style. The lady's voice was full of snobbish awe. I had an impression (perhaps totally superficial) that "pampering" would be the right word to describe the non-Indians' treatment of the Indians. I may be wrong, and it would be enlightening to hear what the Indians have to say. Anyway, in Europe and especially Eastern Europe, people still believe that today's Indians are human wreckages filled with melancholic dignity, squatting in front of their miserable adobe huts wrapped proudly in old blankets, starving, or getting nostalgically drunk. But the reality is rather what I saw in the lobby of La Fonda, the most elegant hotel in Santa Fé: an old Indian woman, not too well washed, lolling in the best leather armchair in the middle of the hall; in front of her on the floor, a dirty (but stylish) cloth; on it, some folklore tourist souvenirs; around her, wealthy ranchers in ten-gallon hats, smiling forbearingly, conciliatorily, and apologetically, as if trying to forget visibly what the woman's ancestors did to theirs and vice versa. The Indians are the big fashion in the southwest: they are referred to as "our forefathers"; their architecture and art is considered "our American art heritage"; women use the metaphor: "He is as good looking as an ancient Apache. . . ."

Taos, Tesuque, San Ildefonso

Three weeks in the United States convinces me that I am in the midst of the mightiest matriarchal society in history. American women are a frightening social, political, and moral force of a still indeterminate range of influence. But with the Pueblos, I understand that this state of affairs might be reason for optimism. The Tewa Indians, once the most powerful masters of the endless boundaries of Rio Grande Valley, forbade their women to enter the *Kiva*—a place of honour to the Pueblo, where men sat and smoked their pipes. And now—where are the Tewas? And where are the Americans, who humble themselves in front of every woman entering an elevator, or at the occasion of every divorce? The Moslems, once the rulers of half of Asia and Africa, considered (logically) that a woman was inferior; the Europeans considered her (quite idiotically) superior. The totally illogical result of the story is well known—and rather sad for the Moslems. In Zanzibar women were not allowed to handle money as it was believed that their touch made it dirty. In America, people (stupidly) give their salaries to their wives. And who now has the Chase Manhattan Bank? The Zanzibarians?

Phoenix, Arizona

A dinner party conversation:

A LADY: "Are there cacti in Poland?"
ME: "No. But we import them."
SHE: "Why?"
ME: "We use the needles for the sewing machines."
SHE: "You're kidding . . ."
ME: "Not at all. We are a small, backward, underdeveloped country."
SHE (after serious thought): "Where do you get them? From Arizona?"

ME: "No. From Soviet Russia, of course."
SHE: "Have they cacti? In Russia?"
ME: "No. But they manufacture them. Industrially."
SHE: "Well, why not? Today anything's possible."

We each had a slight touch of madness in our eyes after a while. But we learned something from our talk.

❧ *Before leaving Phoenix*, a man I respect remarked: "You found people here sympathetic because you belong to a struggling minority in your country, and we too are an intellectual minority struggling for something better. . . ." I agreed with a sigh. The difference is that here, they at least have a chance to win.

FLAGSTAFF, ARIZONA. GRAND CANYON

I saw several interesting things. To enumerate:

1) A TV broadcast of the discussion on Vietnam by the Senate's Foreign Relations Committee. I'm not a historian, but I can't recall a similar event in the world's political history: the leaders of a great nation speaking simply and openly about the most crucial and complicated problems of the moment—as if they wish to feed the enemy propaganda. But in the United States, you may say everything against the government, and it does no damage; whereas in a Communist state you can say nothing against the government, which harms it extremely.

2) I went to see the Grand Canyon; it took me a day's travel by air and by car to reach it. It is said that the Grand Canyon is Phoenix's main tourist curiosity. One must admit that it's a good-looking chasm, but generally I am not interested in nature for itself. Ten minutes of admiration are enough for the greatest marvels; then nature can be interesting only as a background for something else.

3) I saw Hopi Indians dancing. They may be the only race totally shaped by literature. Is there a better example

of mendacious embellishment than what literature did for the Indians? In reality, they are fat, funny, and have terribly thin arms. If that's so now when they eat well, how must they have looked in times when they ate poorly and were tubercular. Yet literature describes their statuary features and members.

4) In Flagstaff's Greyhound station, two drunken Indians annoyed everyone around but were nice to me. Probably, in some metaphysical way, they recognized that I belong to another nation with a powerful alcoholic tradition. The principle works in reverse with the buses; they never stop where I am waiting; probably the drivers sense I have the passport of a Marxist country in my pocket.

LOS ANGELES, CALIFORNIA

In one of Émile Zola's novels, the hero stands at the window of a train approaching Paris; the hero contemplates the roofs of the capital and vows to master the city, to conquer it. He was fortunate not to come to Los Angeles. How is it possible to conquer a city where even decent sight-seeing is impossible. Just leaving my hotel I feel lost—the distance to the nearest drugstore is the same as between two villages in France. One's helplessness in such vastness is paralyzing. In a car with an attractive girl, I said: "Let's go somewhere out of town . . . ," having in mind eventual kissing. "But where?" she asked. "Oh, no matter where . . . ," I smiled, trying to hide my intentions, ". . . where the city ends." "Los Angeles never ends," she said firmly.

❧ *The architecture of Los Angeles* stands out like pimples on very smooth skin. California's landscape is like the most beautiful complexion, but all those false Gothic churches, Romanesque chapels, old English manor houses, bastard Welsh cottages, and Islamic baseball stadiums are blemishes. Somehow this architectural circus does not give an impression of primitive *nouveau riche*, but rather a feeling of refinement and sophistication. The atmosphere here is impregnated with gentle, self-assured skepticism, the fruit of climate, wealth, and the age of that wealth. It's no wonder if we think of gold, oil, and the movie industry.

❧ *During a discussion* of different social and political systems, a native Californian observed: "At last we intellectuals know that there exists neither the ideal nor the absolute. Every human construction is marked by human imperfection. The same applies to the political and social structures. This knowledge makes us philosophical."

I agreed: "Of course. One political system is no better or worse than the next. All are marked by human imperfection. Only in some it's better not to mention it."

❧ *At a dinner party*, a distinguished Negro writer asked me what percent of the population would vote anti-Communist if there were free elections in an Eastern European country, such as Poland, for example. I answered that, in my opinion, elections in a totalitarian state can never be free; but if conditions for free voting were created, if all points of views, not only the Communist one, were presented on radio and TV, and if the average person did not fear any aftermath of persecution, about 85 percent of the population would vote anti-Communist.

"That's impossible!" he exclaimed.

I did not want to contradict him, being unsure whether he might know better than I the political situation in Poland. Life has taught me that the world is full of perfectly-oriented intellectuals and students who know much better than I what is going on in my country, even if they live comfortably on the French Riviera or in California. But he continued in a most astonished tone:

"It's impossible that such a tiny minority runs the vast majority!"

I must admit that this manifestation of political freshness and naiveté was totally unexpected. "Look," I argued, "we in old Europe are accustomed to the simple fact that there are a lot of scientific and extremely helpful instruments which allow even the tiniest minority to suppress every majority, even the largest. Such instruments as machine guns, tanks, wiretapping, secret police, prisons . . ."

He started to shout: "I don't agree with you! It's impossible! It's against any logic!" A young woman sitting next to me tried to calm him. "Listen, Mr. ——," she began. "You shut up . . . ," he threw at her.

"You see," I slipped in, "that's the best method if the minority wishes to run the majority. . . . It's very easy, if one only chooses to use it."

On the other hand, it's some comfort that there are still believers in moral symmetry in politics.

❧ *Hollywood.* This word can be placed next to names like Olympus, Arcadia, Sodom, Rome, Paris. It symbolizes a place where, in certain epochs, everyone wanted to be. Now Hollywood has the charm of the past, perhaps its first real charm. There floats around here a nostalgic memory of one of mankind's most charming dreams, that gives to Hollywood a solid, secure position in the hagiography of our century.

Amazing how many Britons are here. They probably consider Hollywood the property of the entire English-speaking world—and not without reason.

❧ *I met in Hollywood* an intelligent gentleman, who happens to be the vice-president of the Motion Picture Association of America. There's nothing terribly exceptional in the existence of a brilliant vice-president. But I must explain that the functions of the high officials of MPA are those of almighty censors for the film production of this country. And one must admit that it is very difficult for a writer to say of a censor that he is brilliant and intelligent because a natural, emotional relationship exists between censors and writers, the same as that between cruel hunters and hunted deer. Despite this, I had a delightful talk with this gentleman—we spoke about the idiocies of portrayals of Russia in the Western movie industry. He asked if I saw "Dr. Zhivago," and I replied no, but I'd seen Miss Julie Christie's photos which was enough for me to make the firm decision never to see the movie. He said he understood. I added that the funniest thing is that Miss Christie tries to look like the Lara of Pasternak's novel, but one is aware only of her hopeless effort; in the end, she just looks like Miss Christie disguised as Lara with the help of Christian Dior. We agreed that Russia and America are such enormous and complex entities that the truth about them can be perceived only by their own writers. Why do the Faulkners never write about Siberia nor the Sholokhovs about Florida? In this vice-president, I found someone who understood what makes me laugh when I watch "Brothers Karamazov" produced in Hollywood or a Russian movie about American spies and the degenerates of Wall Street.

❧ *Disneyland.* I think that Disneyland is a consequent defeat of positivism. Like every philosophical system that claims to be capable of explaining everything, Mr. Disney's attempt to show everything failed miserably. In today's world, there is no place for the philosophy afraid of pronouncing the words: "I do not know." After German concentration camps and the self-destructive madness of communism, we cannot live without metaphysics. Mr. Disney is probably the last worshiper of deism; in the eighteenth century, he would have been acclaimed by the encyclopedists as a genius. Today, trying to visualize (or symbolize) everything, he makes everything—or more precisely, the American universe—appear impoverished and superficial.

❧ *I have seen* the Watts area. One must admit that racism is imposingly erratic: the Germans hated and exterminated the Jews because the latter were (presumably) more capable, more intelligent, well organized, and so on. The Negroes are hated and persecuted in the South because they are (allegedly) illiterate, less intelligent, antisocial, and so on. Probably racism is simply the most primitive human hatred of complexity. And what can be more complex than someone being different from us?

❧ *Things are better* in America than in the rest of the world. The wages are better, the highway network is better, the gasoline is better, the hospitals, elevators, supermarkets, airports, and fertilizers are better. The world has an equal chance only where human qualities enter the competition—such as beauty, virtue, wisdom, knowledge, *esprit.*

SAN FRANCISCO, CALIFORNIA

I have wanted to know this city since my early childhood. San Francisco has the most widespread legend of any American city: its landscape, gold rush, the famous harbor and its pleasures, and Jack London. The last is perhaps the most powerful element of San Francisco's fame. London may be considered a second-rate writer here, yet he did more for America—and contributed more to timeless American propaganda—than all American nineteenth (with the possible exception of Fenimore Cooper) and twentieth century writers combined. The force with which he ingrained his own dreams and desires in the minds and hearts of several generations has no comparison in American literature; it is an unusual literary achievement to make the names of Golden Gate, Sausalito, Oakland, the property of fourteen-year-old boys around the world. After my arrival, I went to Fisherman's Wharf; there are old ships lying there as museum pieces. My God, what magic Jack London had! It was the recapitulation of my most intimate boyhood. San Francisco Bay, the deck of *Wapama,* an old schooner named *L. A. Thayer*—how strangely a child's dreams fit reality here! It all came back to me at once, the simple combinations of words, landscape, and the smell of sea-food; the modern versions of the legendary Greek oyster pirates in the rich Greek restaurant owners along the Embarcadero. How deep Jack London is in all of us with his uncomplicated world of simple emotions and simple glory. . . .

Squaw Valley, California

Europeans know that human needs are flexible. Americans don't. Americans think that human needs are stiff, sacred, and settled once and for ever. It is a great idea; indeed, one that has a big future.

Lake Tahoe, California

An evening with friends in their home on Lake Tahoe. We drank vodka in the Polish way, paying careful attention to each other. We spoke about "third communism," or Eastern European communism, which has differed so from Soviet or Chinese communism. For an Eastern European, it is like speaking about integral or differential calculus to people who have just started to learn algebra. They can't understand that Mr. Gomulka did not come to save Poland or to make life better there, but that he came to save Communism in Poland and to make the Communist structure of power more solid. When I tell them that there is a modern Monroe Doctrine which creates a sphere of indifference east of the Elbe—they stare at me with disbelief.

SACRAMENTO, CALIFORNIA

I've read in *Sacramento Bee* that ". . . Sacramento ranks eighth among cities which in 1964 were most dangerous for women in the number of rapes per capita . . ."

Why—per capita?

SAUSALITO, CALIFORNIA

I was driving from San Francisco with a young student. I asked what he was studying. Political science, he answered. I ventured that after his studies he would choose a career as a diplomat. He denied it. I said he might want to write about politics, economy, history, or follow scientific research. He replied, not at all. I shyly pointed out that his knowledge could be useful in business, but he contemptuously shrugged his shoulders. Then I asked what he was going to do afterwards, and he said he intended to start biochemistry. I said one studies for practical purposes, unless he has parents able to support him endlessly. If not, he must make money in some way. "Oh, that's what you're driving at," he smiled. "My parents don't give me one nickel for my schooling. Until now I've been too busy to think my future over. But in this country that is not the *main* problem. . . ."

SAN FRANCISCO

San Francisco seems a powerful stronghold of British civilization. Nowhere in the United States have I seen so many wares "from England" in display windows, so many English names of fame in the field of shoemaking, nor so many English knobs at entrance doors. How did all this "Englishness" come here? Surely not across the continent. Rather by sea. Rows of wooden façades originating in Glasgow and Hull prove that many British sailors simply felt too tired to go back home around Cape Horn. In that way, San Francisco got its British sense of décor.

BERKELEY, CALIFORNIA

I have been meeting with professors from the English Department at Berkeley, among them a well-known California poet. They complained of the lack of a concentrated literary *milieu* in America, the lack of literary "cafés," an institution in Europe. They feel dissatisfied without contact with other writers, without discussion. They find "literary life" very stimulating and creative. I told him I don't miss my fellow writers at all, and I don't think any contact with them necessary for me. American writers should be happy and thank God every day they are so far away from one another. Generally, where there is enough space, and where writers have little in common (or never meet), there grows and flourishes great literature, as in the last century in Russia. In Warsaw we have literary "cafés" and literary discussions, but neither Dostoevski nor Faulkner were born there. The professors seemed unconvinced.

STANFORD; PALO ALTO, CALIFORNIA

Even among trained Kremlinologists in this country, there persists a common belief that the upper class in Communist society is made up of party members, government officials, high-ranking military people, and industrial managers. Nothing could be further from the truth; these people are the rulers: those overburdened with work, gross, coarse, very limited, "half-or-quarter" intelligent (as we call them), undemanding where a better life is concerned. They live modestly, work fourteen hours a day and are early victims of heart disease. The real upper class are those who serve them—the cynical intellectuals, writers, artists, journalists who sell a preparedness for every lie in return for money and lack of responsibility. Such an attitude is highly profitable in Communist countries. They get in exchange material prosperity, extensive travel to the West paid by the state, intensive sexual *dolce vita,* made possible by their exceptional social position. What is most humorous is that Western Kremlinologists consider them open-minded, progressive allies, the future threat to Marxian orthodoxy; their cynicism is interpreted by American political scientists as liberalism, their vulgar search after worldly wealth, as intellectual refinement. Innocent, naive Westerners! They can't understand that the upper class under communism is the most embittered foe of freedom, of the West, of America—simply because they would be unable to live in a world of free competition.

SAN FRANCISCO

The fire brigade is the darling of Americans; one has only to see their eyes when the fire brigade is in action, no matter whether it's needed or not. The fire brigade embodies the dearest dreams of the American male: speed, noise, cleverness, adroitness—and all in the service of society.

❧ *I saw* a strange street parade. Japanese Catholic youth marched through San Francisco's Market under an American banner and in blue jeans, swinging trumpets and sticks to the beat of European military music with British pageantry. Tiny, fragile youths, whose features were a dissonance in this picture. What magic of this civilization makes the sons (or, at least, close relatives) of yesterday's bitter enemies march under the emblems of their victors?

❦ *"What is the Third Communism* you speak so much about?" asked an American journalist at a dinner party. I reflected a bit as it is often difficult to explain very simple things to an American journalist; they do less harm when they have to deal with complex problems.

"You see," I said, "when an innocent citizen is arrested or murdered by secret police in Russia or China, he disappears without a trace. In a country like Hungary, Poland, or Yugoslavia, an innocent man can still be jailed or murdered, but he is not lost in the unknown. Everyone speaks of him. That is 'third communism.'"

❦ *The American cultural output* has not been too kind to American women. The American novel, during the last fifty years, pictures her as egoistic, stupid, power-thirsty, anti-sexual, and frigid. American movies make her an idyllic idiot, unrealistically beautiful, terribly sweet, girl-scoutish, probably without ovaries, and suspiciously energetic. American theatre sees in her the inexhaustible source of all possible neuroses, mental deviations, and sexual abnormalities. On the other hand, Europeans of my generation still have in mind the flavor of sugarlike puritanism à la Louisa May Alcott. Instead the American woman is, like every woman in the world, the way her men *want* her to be. The enormous mistake of the American male until recently was that he liked to go to bed, but he did not like to stay there. This simple circumstance made the American woman frigid, idiotically beautiful, and neurotic. The last twenty years have changed all that. Coming here, I was sure I was falling into a mixture of obsolete puritanism and the neurotic restraint of instincts and passions. What nonsense! Everybody here has an affair with the wife of his best friend— triangles and quadrangles multiply all over the country. I immediately felt at home.

❧ *I can't get used to the idea* that songs like Irving Berlin's *Cheek to Cheek* or Kern's *Smoke Gets in Your Eyes* mean something different here from that in Europe, where they symbolize the charm of worldly life, the essence of fashionable dreams about chic hotels, the main element of secondhand, cinematic hedonism of the century. Here in California they are folklore.

❧ *I was invited* to a party. There were some writers, scholars, musicians, and a beautiful Negro girl. A very talented actress, I was told. She was gentle, charming, intelligent, and, as far as I could see, adored by her friends and everyone around. We left together: she gave me a ride to my hotel. In the car she said: "You will never know how hard it is to be a Negro in America . . ."

BERKELEY, CALIFORNIA

Berkeley is full of (in Eastern European eyes) comical Marxian fans or Communist *aficionados* who form a strange school of dialectical idealism, probably under the pressure of the name of the place. One of those guitar-playing hippie First Church disciples said to me: "Communism is a wonderful, noble idea; it is pure and most human in concept. Last of all it can be reduced to the simplest and most beautiful demand that all men should be brothers."

"Maybe that is the trouble with it," I said. "Maybe it would have been wiser to call men to be cousins, at least for the first few years after every revolution. Brothers are more informal with each other and find it easier to kill one another."

ABOARD THE *California Zephyr*—
NEVADA, UTAH, COLORADO

When we sit in Europe in a cinema and watch a western in technicolor, we are inclined to mock the artificiality of the colors. Utah and Nevada seen from Vista-Dome cars are entirely in technicolor, proving that even Hollywood movies have some realism.

The haphazard meetings in dining cars are very difficult to handle. They always start with enthusiasm.

"Where are you from?"

"From Poland, in Europe."

"Oh, how beautiful (interesting, exciting, fascinating —it depends on the individual predisposition to enthusiasm) . . .!"

"Not so exceptionally fascinating, Madame. A country like many others."

"Really? Is that so? Tell me, what sports do they play?"

"All games, Madame, known in the civilized world."

"Do they play golf?"

"No, Madame, rather not . . ."

"Do they play baseball?"

"No, I'm afraid not, because of . . ."

"Do they play football?"

"Yes, but it is rather a game like football called soccer . . ."

"You see, I always thought that Poland must be different and strange . . ."

I should feel crushed, but as I am a devoted reader of *Winnie the Pooh,* I know what happened to Tigger when he wanted to defend the good fame of the tigers.

CHICAGO, ILLINOIS

New York is opulence, decadence, and culture. The southwest is grandeur, space, and future. California is wealth, epicureanism, and luxuriance. Chicago is strength. Dark strength and real power. Here in Illinois I first understood exactly why the Confederacy was doomed to lose in the Civil War. The reasons are still visible and perceptible a hundred years later.

This is America as Europeans of my generation imagined it to be. A genuine American urban landscape, an immense wilderness of fire escapes, engraved deeply in our memories during the Twenties. Tough, filthy, and great. One can imagine the merciless and heroic struggles when this city was the prize. It must be the only place where all that happened here in the Twenties *could* have happened.

❧ *Chicago's Old Town.* A special display of good taste turned into bad taste. An artistic Coney Island. Americans are the victims of their own capacity for reproduction. It is frightening—the American ability to spoil everything by ceaseless multiplication, the possibility of producing every value in antihuman amounts.

❧ *Hotel Atlantic.* I would miss something of Chicago if I had not stayed here. The plushy shabbiness, the bygone splendor of the Twenties. All the heroes of the dirty and brutal struggle for power, headed by Al Capone, came to mind. Chicagoans do not like any mention of the Twenties; they consider this period shameful. They are wrong. What actually counts is the impact of a legend; its moral background or implications are secondary. No matter if Chicagoans wish it or not, their city remains a symbol of the bloody facts of the Twenties, and it would be better to turn that legend into a cultural value, taking care not to slip into the opposite extreme of pride. Such pride would be more shameful than today's ambiguous discretion; shops would stock Al Capone skull-ashtrays.

❧ *If I have to explain* what communism is to an average American, I deliberately use a technical metaphor to appeal to their pragmatic, engineer-like imagination. "Communism," I say, "is like a damaged or broken engine or a plumbing installation. No one knows how to repair it. But it runs and people are obliged to use it."

"Oh!" sighs the American, "it must be hell!"

Detroit, Michigan

Aboard the plane someone asked what I think about women. I answered that I do not think about them; I like them, or I love them. "But," he insisted, "you have to have a judgment. Everybody has."

"That's right," I said, "but when I start thinking about women, I stop loving or even liking them."

This man was certain that Europeans do not know much about women because we do not think about them. He's wrong.

❧ *River Rouge Plant.* The name "Ford" is today as familiar to every living man as Moses, Columbus, or Beethoven. Even if someone does not know what Columbus or Beethoven did, he surely has heard their names: they have a timeless place in the human consciousness, reserved for creators and discoverers. The same with Ford: he created a new world, a world of production. Visiting Ford's Rouge Plant, I wasn't sure if he had created a world or a hell. I always imagined "hell" to be a synonym for inhuman precision. Like here, where blue or red plates arrive with a second's exactness at the only point in the universe where they are strictly needed. This hell works with blessed efficiency to produce something most human beings desire (the perennial function of hell—to produce objects of human desire!). In any case, it is better that people here do not realize what an automobile means for the citizen of a Communist country. To possess a car, he is willing to betray, steal, and humiliate himself. It is the peak of his ambitions. It's amusing to think about it in Detroit, where half of the world's cars are produced. What a source for moral bribery. . . .

❧ *Jefferson–Jackson Dinner of the Democratic party of Michigan.* This kind of political gathering is more amusing here than in Europe: a couple of drinks before make people happier and a little bit noisy. The speakers can hardly be heard. It all makes politics more personal, a matter of digestion rather than conviction.

In front of Cobo Hall there are two demonstrations: one against the war in Vietnam, and one for it. One gets an impression that the substantial diversity of opinion among Americans has something to do with hygiene. The unkempt and not-too-well-washed are against, the very neat are "pro" (which, of course, has nothing in common with moral evaluation!). I think the only one to blame for this war and the following dissent is Jean Jacques Rousseau: two centuries ago he made Americans believe that human beings are basically good. The result has been a myriad of unforeseen complications.

❧ *It is a matter* of prestige here to pull American television to pieces. It takes little effort indeed to criticize its intellectual shallowness, the commonplace routine, artistic monotony, primitive insipidness of its entertainment. Contempt for TV is a characteristic of American intelligentsia, slandering TV a favorite pastime. One important fact is overlooked, namely, that American show business plunges deeper every year into self-established classicism. It is no longer healthy, earthy, folksy, dynamic and popular art, linked with thousands of ties to the real and the actual. In the last few years it has acquired some of the features of the ancient Greek spectacles, or baroque theatre of seventeenth-century European courts, or Japanese Kabuki theatre. These forms are characterized by set rules and a highly stylized manner which constitute criteria to estimate the degree of perfection of the content, which is always written, filmed, and staged according to stock convention. We know unerringly, with no possibility of surprise, how Batman will act, what will happen to Superman, who is who in Bonanza, what Dr. Kildare is going to say in any given situation, how the Munsters,

Donald Duck, Popeye the Sailor will react, even which musical phrase will end a number by the Supremes. What keeps us in suspense is the degree of quality inside the circle of classic categories, the evaluation of performance within stiffly-established principles. TV critics' rage makes them forget that the petrifaction of a spectacle's convention is *not* synonymous with the diminishing of its attractiveness; audiences in Greek and Roman amphitheaters and admirers of *commedia dell'arte* knew this perfectly well.

❧ *I was invited* to attend the Economic Club of Detroit luncheon. The speaker was Mr. Ronald Reagan, candidate for Governor of California. Somebody asked me what I thought of Brezhnev. "He is handsome," I answered. "Of course, in a Russian way."

"But that can't be a political opinion," smiled my collocutor.

"Why not?" I wondered. "Kennedy was handsome. Lindsay is handsome. Something positive links good looks and politics. Besides, the difference between Brezhnev's good looks and that of Lindsay's is very symbolic and suggests the difference in quality between Russia and America."

My partner looked at me suspiciously. "And Mr. Ronald Reagan," he said, "isn't he handsome too?"

❧ *Pragmatism and materialism* shaped American history and modern society. But this society always has a second face, determined by conscious idealism and awareness of its own moral mission—if not always precise, always sincere and deep. The Quakers and Woodrow Wilson, UNRRA and the Peace Corps—these are some of the embodiments of a superbly-organized, technological, and socially-scientific apostolate. After 150 years of practice, Americans have scored many valuable achievements.

I met a gentleman in Detroit who until his thirty-fifth year never left Ohio, but his five sons are now all over the world—in Ethiopia, Venezuela, Thailand, Polynesia, and Greece, serving as workers of philanthropic or scientific organizations in aid programs. I think that after all the obstacles, drawbacks, and misunderstandings, such activity will result in a powerful American universalism.

Of course, another American universalism already exists—that of moods. I doubt if there is anyone now in his forties who did not whistle, hum, get sentimental, dance, or kiss a girl and did not recall it later to the sound of *Star Dust* or *The Man I Love*. Today, the universe of emotions and sensations is constructed on the law of communicating mediums with the help of Gershwin, Irving Berlin, and Hoagy Carmichael.

WASHINGTON, D.C.

After heat in Houston, biting cold in Santa Fé, dryness in Phoenix, icy rain in Chicago, and snow in Detroit, the spring weather in Washington seems to be as serene as the State Department's highest officials.

I met a well-known political columnist. He complained about not living in Europe. It is amusing that members of the European intelligentsia want to live in America, and the American intelligentsia dream about living in Europe. This no longer makes the sense it did in the times of Henry James, T. S. Eliot, Gertrude Stein, Hemingway, F. Scott Fitzgerald, and Henry Miller. Then, Europe was still producing the Prousts, the G. B. Shaws, the Picassos, the Manns, and still fulfilled its reputation for intellectual hegemony now completely past. Europeans prefer Hitchcock to Godard, a good western to boring *cinéma d'oeil*, and Tennessee Williams to Duerrenmatt. Only American snobs maintain that Robbe-Grillet is more interesting than Philip Roth, that Moravia knows life better than Saul

Bellow, and that John Ford is childish but Alain Resnais mature.

❧ *Even if we accuse* American TV of certain ossification of artistic content, we have to admit that this imperfection is highly compensated for by the TV commercial, a main hate object of American snobs. American TV is now the cradle of a new branch of art; the commercials are not only the most polished American artistic achievements of the postwar period but also a most important American contribution to the twentieth century cultural image, next to skyscraper architecture and jazz. TV commercials spring from the abundant traditions of American advertising, which in the Thirties already knew how to appeal to human needs and wishes through visual and psychological mastery. The advertising business is an empire built on the most modern techniques of pictorial art in the service of cruelty—experienced when passing along the street in the scorching heat and meeting a huge billboard ad of Ballantine beer; the supernaturalistic, brisk drops on the glass form such an idea of desired coolness that someone thirsty can be led to pathological deeds. TV commercials sublimate those feelings—they create a new, nonexistent world of fantasy and unexpected sensations. All that has been accomplished by the movies, acting, photography, visual gags, animated cartoons, comic strips, and graphic posters during the last fifty years—it all serves. One has to *see* it to know what a source of affection, hope, and concupiscence an ad for frankfurters, aspirin, or toothpaste may be. If the might of art is measured by its degree of influence upon man's feelings, wha inspires feelings is artistic. But to explain the TV com mercial by sensual appeal only would be unfair. Amer cans have succeeded in creating an ideal, surreali universe, moved by its own logic, ordered by its ow aesthetics. They have "dematerialized" the world of things, given life to objects, and transformed them into ideas. Nobody has ever seen *such* a hamburger because it doesn't exist in reality, but what a delight to look at!

❧ *Today I tried to convince* a high army officer that if America is going to win over Russia, it will not be due to more powerful rockets but to more powerful cleansers for washing dishes. Industrial and scientific priority make the American housewife the world's mightiest housewife—a most important, historical victory over communism. He wasn't sure I was right.

❧ *If in a Communist country* you expect a delivery and it arrives, you are pleasantly surprised; you never counted on it. Between two social partners, the one who orders and the one who takes the order, no moral relationship exists. In America, if by some incredible unlikelihood, an expected delivery does not arrive, one is frightened; some moral irregularity has been perpetrated. If democracy is to defeat communism, it is mainly on the basis of its social solidity. In America, even the smallest cell of the social organism pulsates with life and consciousness and automatically bears responsibility toward the whole social body. That makes the entire organism healthy. Under communism, the only part of the social organism that really functions, hectically and effectively, is the brain—the disposal center. The rest is inactive, almost paralyzed; the single cells do not have any force to live and to respond. The brain, tired from the lack of help, tormented by feverishly-made decisions, commits mistakes, mistakes, mistakes. . . .

❧ *This epoch* I consider as marked by the total failure of youth—in a most universal sense. In the history of mankind, youth has never been conspicuously clever. It has always thought itself much more interesting than it really was. But today's youth is stupider than ever, because it makes adolescence an ideal, a way of life, and attributes to it rights, privileges, qualities, and virtues (of both brain and soul) that are purely fictitious, artificially invented, and phony. Being young is the most fleeting human condition—a fact that is terribly humiliating to any young person who thinks about it. The inability to recognize this simple truth immerses contemporary youth in the ridiculous. One hundred and fifty years ago, the Romanticists—Byron, Pushkin, de Musset, Mickiewicz—glorified adolescence as a state of supersensitivity but, at the same time, were very humble and melancholic about the value of youth. As an ideal solution they proposed dying young —and many of them did it, which isn't at all the case of today's juvenile ideologists: many of them have already reached their forties and believe it worthy only to prolong the adolescent look, habits, and manners in the most comical way. American youth is neither worse nor more stupid than any other in the western world; its only idiotic feature is that it misses its fiducial mark. American youth alone in the world cannot cast much reproach on its elders. It has inherited from them a well-functioning social and economic system (that can still be improved, of course, but by no means needs to be destroyed first) wealth, freedom, and an enormous, main luxury, severely forbidden other (for example, Communist) societies: namely allowance to be contemptuous of one's elders.

❧ *A Polish friend* visiting America said once: "At home in Warsaw, I'm going to repeat that the American working class is deprived of roofs over their heads. Chiefly when they sit in convertibles."

❧ *Intellectual, artistic, and cultural nonconformity* have increased here in recent years to such an extent, socially and statistically, that there is a new conformity. Uniqueness is the most common, current feature. Being different means to be like everybody. Every American, every city, every product, every nightclub, every shop wants to be amazingly (!) different. Of course, the uncontrollable desire to be different breeds a new uniformity, as has happened to hippies and Beatloids of all kinds: everyone has the same hairdo, and their blue jeans are torn in exactly the same way. This equality of intention is, in my opinion, much more thoughtless and humiliating than the brand equality of American middle class, white-collar workers. The latter find a joy in being alike—in having the same solid shoes, the same hats, the same way of laughing, and the same exclamations. I must admit that, watching them leave their banks and offices, I was many times attracted by their "alikeness"—the breed of their clothes and manners make them attractive to anyone from behind the Iron Curtain. The Communists, in spite of all their efforts, cannot achieve the goal of their "mass society" dreams: that average citizens would enjoy being the same as other average citizens. The quality of Communist "alikeness" is so poor that everyone hates it.

What makes the efforts of hippies and all spectacular nonconformists so fruitless is the supernatural American capacity for production. All here is mass-produced in a flash, everything undergoes the stupefying process of reproduction, superproduction, and overproduction, the process of improving and multiplying every object in hundreds of colors, classes, versions and shapes *with* "something" or without. Is there a need for nonconformity on the market? Individuality is in demand? The industry responds immediately, and limitless kinds, sorts, and brands of nonconformity and individuality are furnished to the department stores. Millions of girls wear millions of badges with the inscription: "I am different." The most ambitious swinger who yesterday invented the newest and most extravagant haircut or shirt design today sees his idea on the street, multiplied a thousandfold by imitation, manufactured and distributed through the night by industry, commerce, and the mass media. Of course, the same applies to the world of thought, ideas, and the latest accomplishments in literature and art.

❧ *Today I saw* on TV how a modern American mother interrogates her daughter about a newly acquired "beau": "How is he?" she asks impatiently. "Does he have personality?"

Don't honesty, appearance, education, social position, or even money count any longer on the market of human values? Is it so?

❧ *It is neither might*, nor power, nor magnitude, nor space, nor limitless resources of wealth that characterizes America. America of today is first of all marked by diversity. If this country is to be submerged by a suicidal catastrophe, created by itself and originating in itself, it will be by the incredible variety of things developed by its capacity for production. I can imagine a holocaust of excess, of surplus—a consequence of unlimited productive output. "What kind of potatoes do you like?" ask waiters in every restaurant. "Fried, whipped, mashed, trampled, kicked, curled or boiled? Russian style, Lebanese style, from North Ireland, or through a Puerto Rican strainer?" "What kind of slacks are you looking for?" asks the subversive sales clerk. "Long, short, middle? With cuffs or not? Buttoned or zipped? How many pockets? And in which of the 137 colors we can sell you?" It is the same with aircraft, salads, life insurance, and shampoo. There is a danger in this frightening multitude, in this multiplication of everything into an infinity of versions, and the crazy determination to exhaust *every* possibility of life. This in the end, as we know, is impossible. We can easily confirm it with the example of greeting cards. I must admit that shops with greeting cards have made me more optimistic, though filling me with disgust. They demonstrate the uselessness of the efforts of those who intend to master the entirety of life with the help of flawlessly planned production. Manufacturers of greeting cards pretend to fulfill all the needs of all people as far as greetings are concerned; they produce cards for Easter, Christmas, New Years, and for every possible holiday of every existing creed, classified for all stages of human existence—age, status of family, society, education. There are greetings for birthdays, weddings, and promotions, for fathers, mothers, grandpas, cousins, and adopted children. Everything seems scheduled, and if we look carefully, we find greetings for an unexpected visit, a premature pregnancy, a passed exam in anthropology, or a mutual divorce agreement. It seems the manufacturers have foreseen every possible contingency, but I always had trouble finding a card I liked, which is extremely comforting. Nor could I ever find a plain, unprinted card whereon to inscribe my own greetings, evidence of the manufacturers' fear of human invention.

This excess leads to the lack of concrete facts or decisions. Needs and demands become unsettled, rotted by perennial hesitation. Both under communism and here, one is unable to buy a pair of slacks: there, because not enough can be produced; here, because too many are produced. If one goes to a department store with the firm resolve to buy a certain kind of slacks, he won't; he faces such an inhuman variety of slacks that his notion of need gets confused. Suddenly, all of the slacks fit his idea, destroying and annihilating his conception. Consequently, one no longer knows whether what he looks on, or holds in his hand, is really what he needed and wanted. The infernal sabbat of colors, shapes, and types kills the joy of the wish. In the end, the human being is deprived both of the necessity of searching and the happiness of finding. And that *is* a danger.

❦ *I was perhaps unjust* and too rough on American youth. Most young people here have two interesting qualities:

1) they are more intelligent than their elders (the merit of the American educational system or of an eternal ruling that youth is better oriented to current reality; that does *not* mean wiser . . .); and

2) they've tried to destroy, in recent years, the idolatry of money in this society.

Money is no more the main aspiration of rising generations, no more the overwhelming element in social striving. The reason behind it (perhaps neither very idealistic nor moral) is that it is already more difficult to be interestingly poor in this country than to be averagely prosperous. Being broke has much more to do with extravagance than with bad luck. In any case the young take the credit for some hopes.

DRIVE THROUGH MARYLAND

In the modern American landscape, Howard Johnson's is the campanile of the village church.

BETHESDA, MARYLAND

To escape the noise and lack of privacy of a big-city dwelling, American genius created suburbia—which became but one more proof that the incapability of escaping is inherent in the human condition. A single lawn mower has the noise power of 10 neighborhood cocktail parties.

BOSTON, MASSACHUSETTS

Boston is old, ugly, dirty, and yet extremely elegant. Everything is inferior here: the pavements, rest rooms and transportation—but at the same time better than anywhere. Contradiction? Paradox? Not at all. It is the natural superiority of culture over civilization. The waterfront in Cambridge I find marvelous, but I am afraid many would consider it gloomy and hideous.

❧ *I sat on a bench* and looked at the Common when an elderly gentleman in tartan waistcoat asked me a question. When I answered in my not-too-well-polished English, he asked: "You are from the South, aren't you? Texas or Arizona, is that not so?"

How strange! This country does not accept the possibility of one being an alien. . . .

CAMBRIDGE, MASSACHUSETTS

American universities are replete with American scientists devoting their lives to scrutinizing, analyzing, and evaluating communism, its history, exploits, accomplishments, and failures. I have been asked what I think of them.

"They are terrific," I answered. "Their research power, theoretical knowledge, and its effects are imposing. They seem to know everything. However, I can imagine how their tremendous effort will go to waste."

"What do you mean?"

"You see, for instance, that they know virtually everything about hoggery. They've collected dramatic statistics and mastered with tantalizing precision all the available information about the quality and characteristics of porkmeat. They have data about Communist pigs that people in Eastern Europe have no idea about. But the people there know one thing the Kremlinologists remain totally ignorant of. Namely—how to find and buy a slice of ham."

❦ *First Church in Cambridge.* It stimulates neither the imagination nor religious fervor. But the words to the left of the pulpit—"In the Love of Truth and in the Spirit of Jesus We Unite for the Worship of God and the Service of Man"—still possesses the iron strength of the cautious faith that shaped an industrial society and mass education.

❦ *In my hotel,* allegedly the best in Cambridge, I complained of the nocturnal inferno in the heating pipes. "If you have warmth in your room," explained the clerk at the desk, "it proves that there is central heating at work. Heating means pipes, and pipes make noise." I have to admit I was impressed by the infallibility of Harvard's school of philosophy, but some ontological questions remained unanswered.

❦ *My luncheon partners* discussed the involvement of intelligence agencies in American public and academic life in a rather condemning and upset tone, of course. "You won't believe," said one, "what enormous sums of money the CIA spends for scientific research in this country, how many scientists they support, how much they give for foundations and grants."

"Blessed country," I thought. "Has the only secret police in history which does not take, but gives, money to those it is supposed to watch . . ."

PROVIDENCE, RHODE ISLAND;
NEW LONDON, CONNECTICUT

I was supposed to explore the New England landscape through the windows of the train from Boston to New Haven, but the windows were so dirty it was impossible to enjoy the charms of the country. It is rather difficult to explore America by railway.

NEW HAVEN, CONNECTICUT

Yale, a place that makes us long for a calm dignity of thought in the shade of respectable, safeguarding, perennial wisdom, as P. G. Wodehouse would say, or Anatole France, or probably both of them, which is Yale's merit. I never saw such an explosion of false Gothic, phony Romanesque, and secondhand Classicism that, instead of repelling by falseness, inspires respect, recognition, and sentimental appreciation.

❧ *On every campus*, I meet bright young men who say, "We are the first American generation to avail ourselves of the privilege of rebelling, of the right to criticize, and so we are accused of being leftist, Communist, or God knows what. But all we want is to improve on the status quo." Or "This nation is divided between anti-Communists and liberals. The first are obsessed by the conviction that every attempt to change society equals communism."

Later, they take me for a ride through the countryside —usually through the poverty-ridden sections, most of them Negro slums. As I look at the deteriorating buildings, they watch me carefully for a reaction of horror at the sight of such misery. But the misery doesn't impress me; I've seen worse in my own country. This misery is brighter than ours; the children run around in blue jeans, which are the dream of prosperous children in Poland. What does impress me is the bright young men themselves—their sensitivity and compassion. Their counterparts in my homeland don't give a damn about such problems; either they're indifferent to them or they're convinced that any effort toward improving them would be in vain. What does impress me is that this society is not resigned to its shameful imperfections but is concerned about them, that its youth is busy creating conditions in which it can carry on the fight against them. When I say that the same poverty and misery exist in Communist Europe, I am not always believed. Of course, no one in Warsaw or Moscow would dare show an American what is shown to me here. It is forbidden; our bright young men risk being arrested if they insist on showing visitors our social blights.

NEW YORK

Entry into New York from the northeast. The overwhelming awareness of bulk, magnitude, and namelessness. One is immediately conscious of how easy it is to disappear without leaving a trace within that immensity, and to perish the same way. A human being is without any chance in this maelstrom of a metropolis if he does not have luck on his side.

❧ *After one has crossed America,* New York makes a strange impression. It seems bigger than all the rest of the country put together. I don't even know in precisely what sense. Whenever I arrive, I feel attacked from all sides by the configuration of vertical shapes, lines and cubes that makes the beauty of this city. The beauty of most cities derives either from the sense of proportion conveyed, the pageant of rationalism provided, or the sumptuousness of their décor. The beauty of New York derives from its rage for construction. That rage proving itself more triumphant than anything else in this century.

❧ *The fact* that there are as many weary, sad, colorless and shabby-looking people in the United States as elsewhere is very little known in the rest of the world. The big legend still consists of the widespread conviction that the tired do not exist here. In spite of all means of communication, the color slide is still the most powerful source of knowledge about America. The slide and the legend are relics of letters from relatives who were not doing badly. In the eyes of Europeans everybody has succeeded here, because the poor measure the success of others not by the work put in but by its spectacular effects, and those are quite spectacular in their American manifestations. It's like another legend spread in Europe —that Americans do not clean their clothes but simply throw them away, and this is the reason for many of the American aid programs to Europe during the first half of the century. Here on the spot, one notices that the cleaning, mending, and laundry businesses are among the mightiest.

🌺 *Central Park.* Saturday at noon, some teen-agers are at an outdoor music shell—mainly girls between twelve and sixteen. In the shell, a very mediocre big-beat combo plays rock'n'roll and rhythm-and-blues. On the stage are three girls of about fifteen but very well-developed in bust and hips. They are dancing, although their "frugging" or "monkeying" is rather like a collected sample of semisexual gestures in their comical exaggeration than dancing. It looks like awkward training for the future. Some dozen younger girls dance frantically around the shell, repeating the poses of the three on the stage; these younger girls are far less rounded and shaped, quite thin and miserable. Mothers and relatives look on approvingly. This generation will probably realize in the most radical way all that *Playboy* is fighting for so valiantly. Two things attract my attention:

1) the opulent girls on the stage are stimulated in their juvenile exhibitionism by small, perhaps ten-year-old, boys who torment themselves with drums, guitars and singing—it reminds one of the old, Oriental use of infantile eunuchs in medieval harems; and

2) this approach to sex is like the heavy preparation

of a sports team to perform a game or match, a simple training to fulfill some physical duties in the most skilful way.

But sexual life is neither physical duty nor a matter of measured performance like track and field. Who is going to tell it to these kids?

❧ *The racial situation* in New York is strange; the Negroes move normally in the streets, no one bothers them, and, as a wanderer from abroad may observe, others are rather considerate of them. But when I wanted to go to Harlem, friends told me not to, that Negroes do not like whites there. I felt as I did in prewar Germany, where in coffee-shops one read "Jews not accepted." Can any racial equality be reached this way? Perhaps it is not racial equality at stake?

❧ *American socialism?* Of course it exists and at every step. As is known, socialism set two goals for itself, never realized in societies ruled by Marxists; one is statistical happiness through the maximal material satisfaction for the largest segment; the other is compulsory social equality or enforcement of the social equality. A young lady, a friend, and I boarded a bus at the Plaza to go down Fifth Avenue. It was Saturday evening. Next to the bus was a Rolls Royce, and inside were two men and a woman. We in the bus moved one yard per hour. The same for the Rolls Royce. We, the girl, the friend, and I, sat very comfortably in the empty bus, not worse off than those in the Rolls. I assumed that we, my friends and the Rolls Royce people, went to dinner. All of us would eat very well, only those in the Rolls would pay more. We were all dressed in the same kind of clothes, only the Rolls Royce people paid more for them. And one did not go forward faster than the other. Isn't that American socialism indeed?

🌺 *The American lower middle class* that forms the statistical backbone of this society and decides its general image is terribly folksy. It adores fancy dresses, gadgets, street parades, paper hats, glittering *réclames*, and hundreds of electric bulbs above every delicatessen shop. Europeans tend to smile mockingly. They are wrong. Every lower middle class adores the same things, but not every one can afford it.

🌺 *Every epoch* has its saints. The Middle Ages had Saint Francis, Saint Thomas Aquinas, and Saint Catherine of Siena. Our epoch has had the Beatles, Frank Sinatra, and Brigitte Bardot. They have had their hagiography, preached every day by newspapers. They also have suffered and considered themselves martyrs. Of course, history is perfectly able to discern some differences between Sinatra and Saint Thomas but, for some time, the Beatles and Bardot shared one of the most exclusive attributes of the saints: adoration. Who is to be blamed for it? Probably our epoch: all of us.

🌺 *In my opinion*, we are now witnessing perhaps the most historic switch in America. The American Negroes may become the most privileged social group of this nation. Why? It is the one social group among many that does not fear the American Negro. With time, more and more often, we will hear Negroes saying: "This one is quite a good, decent Whitey. Let him go his way . . ."

🌺 *At a party*, we discussed the possible panorama of an eventual Russian invasion on this continent. "They can be easily defeated," I said, "in big cities. For example, when they invade New York, all that Americans have to do is to open as widely as possible every entrance to every department store. In half an hour, the whole Russian army is either in Macy's or Alexander's, you shut the entrance door, and they are trapped. You do not need Marines; doormen are enough. They will be so fascinated by mod shirts, toilet paper, and TV dinners that disarmament can be effected by the Bunnies from the neighboring Playboy Club. For the hard-core commissars, it is advisable to increase the stock of bathroom equipment in pink, red, and purple shades."

❧ *The real tragedy* of the Negro problem is that Negroes do not want integration, tolerance, full civil rights, or equal opportunities. They do not want to be accepted, admitted, or respected. They want to be loved, and loved because they are Negroes with four centuries of suffering on their backs. It proves they are impossibly young as a race. We older races know that powerful religions originated in the name of love, religions that ruled millions of souls and whole empires, but with no considerable results. We know that lack of hate is probably the greatest moral achievement mankind may ever hope to attain. Reading James Baldwin in Europe I had an impression of dealing with a rather naive, although very fresh, mode of literary perception. I could not understand it because, on the other hand, Baldwin exhibited much maturity as a writer and as a person. Here in the States, facing and watching the Negroes, I see it at every step, in every bus.

❧ *Americans have succeeded* in an extraordinary accomplishment—they have saturated the planet with the firm conviction that it is most chic to dislike Americans. The Soviets grasped it early, and the main part of their politics and propaganda is built on this American achievement. They've done well everywhere—except in the Soviet bloc.

❧ *I must admit* one mocking reproach that hostile Europeans address towards America is justified. It is the unusual number of people that old wise Jews call *me-shuggener* or the "crackpots" or the "nuts." They are every-where—on the streets, in the buses, in the coffee-shops, brooding around the counter and waiting for the possi-bility of a monologue. Several times a day, I am asked not to sin with women or to be careful about measles, by older, innocent-looking ladies, or by cheerful, filthy gen-tlemen with once-handsome faces and a maniacal glitter behind glasses. I remember the Russian proverb: "He is gone berserk from wealth . . ." Probably it applies to this society. The dilemma is: should a society strive to ac-cumulate big wealth and a formidable proportion of mental disorders? Or is it better to remain poor and sane? It's not up to me to answer.

❦ *Since Russia* started buying American and Canadian wheat, we cannot discuss communism seriously. It seems sheer boorishness to explain this state of affairs by the failure of the kolkhoz system. If the kolkhozes were left alone, they would be able to provide the Soviet Union with all the necessary food, although they produce sta-tistically less than the same agricultural unit before the revolution. But between a kolkhoz and a loaf of fresh baked bread extends the *via dolorosa economica* of com-munism, in which crops get rotten, lost, or perish in a way that could never be explained away with the abject-ness of imperialists and thieves, as was attempted in recent *en vogue* economic show trials.

❦ *The widespread image* of New York as an urban center marked decisively by capitalistic, or rather pluto-cratic, flavor is totally incorrect. New York is folksy; it is a people's city—like ancient Athens, medieval Flor-ence, nineteenth-century Vienna, and timeless Paris. Like London, Berlin, and Moscow never were, because the establishments' voices were there, always more influential, fascinating, and fashionable than those of the people. Of course, folksy cities are much more creative and stimulating and bear more artistic values. The only drawback is that their people turn more easily into mobs.

❦ *At every step,* a member of the New Left tells me that in spite of all doubts and disappointments, it's getting better in Russia. "Look," they say, "at Yevtushenko. He shows that something moves, that things improve. Let's wait, time works for us. . . ." What am I supposed to do? I nod silently. How can I explain to all these naive Marxian-American boy scouts that Yevtushenko is a licensed, nonconformist, professional dissenter; that no one in Russia is allowed to recite his poetry in front of 18,000 listeners without the blessing of the Politburo. If someone makes a good political deal out of such an event, it is for the first rank of the Party and not the free reign of culture. Because if that were the case, such a meeting would never take place. The Party serves itself with many tools: primitive ones like Fadeyev and Kochetov, more complex ones like Ehrenburg, and the newest models like Yevtushenko.

❦ *Lunch at Sardi's* with two world-famous journalists. Very good chicken—old fashioned and baked in the pot. We spoke about America as a land of possibilities. I said that the multitude of possibilities is probably most killing. If I meet a chairman, president, professor, or famous writer and try to make him familiar with some of my circumstances, he always says: "But there are no problems at all. We need people like you here in this country. Enormous possibilities exist. Right now I'll give you the names of various chairmen, presidents, professors, and famous writers who will be delighted to meet you and provide all you need." He gives, I note, and later I try laboriously to visit all of them. It takes time, money, and a lot of effort to locate them, reach them (America is painfully huge), make an arrangement, and finally speak to them. Each is extremely cordial, approachable, and understanding. "Of course," he says, "there are enormous possibilities in this country. Especially for a man like you. Right now I am going to give you some names of people who will be delighted . . ."

This charming way of meeting people has made my travels very pleasant and positively enriched my life.

❧ *At a dinner party,* I expressed some political beliefs.

A young French leftist, who a moment before had attacked de Gaulle violently, verbally dragging him through the mud, asked: "Are you going back to Poland?"

"Are you going back to France?" I asked in return.

"Of course," he replied. "Why not?"

"Then why shouldn't I?"

"Because," he said hesitantly, "you are so definitely against socialism in Poland."

"No more than you are against Gaullism in France," I said. "But I'm not afraid for your future, whereas you are afraid for mine. Doesn't that indicate something about the moral aspects of the two regimes?"

2.

From the Notebook of a Dilettante

DILETTANTISM

While lacking a philosophical, sociological, historical, and political education, I do not cease to meditate upon philosophy, sociology, history, and politics. Consequently, it must be admitted that whatever I turn over in my mind bears a mark of incorrectness. Too, my afterthoughts are consistently inconsistent with these disciplines' accomplishments. Having acquired the habit of exhibiting my thoughts in print, I let myself in for the deserved reproach of dilettantism. However, assuming that both my premises and my conclusions are hazy and precarious, I write them down, nevertheless, and inject them with simple, human experience. For it has never been proved that a dilettante has nothing to say.

BUS EPISTEMOLOGY

I sat on a Third Avenue bus observing a sympathetic, middle-aged woman; she was well groomed, not unappealing, and smelled of middle-income perfume.

She was immersed in a book, its title, clearly exposed—
Diet, Sex and Yoga.

The Statue of Liberty could easily be replaced by this lady with her book as the torch.

MELODRAMATIC REALISM

An important American contribution to contemporary ontology and the modern vision of life is the widespread belief that in America one can always start anew. Only death constitutes a positive end, an absolute and final break. While alive, man not only has a right to, but also the duty of, countless beginnings. Americans appear not to notice this peculiarity in their existence; they accept it as natural. But it doesn't seem natural to persons coming from European or Asian societies and cultures where failures are irreparable. Such melodramatic realism makes a European smile ironically, but his smile is misplaced. Melodramatic changes of fate, new chances, miraculous turnovers of fortunes are still real in this country. It derives, partly, from the common lack of resignation. Resignation, in both its positive and negative meanings, is an unknown state of mind. Three septuagenarian ladies sit on the porch of a Florida hotel, a fourth arrives and greets them with: "Hello, girls . . ." She doesn't joke, she means it; she does not feel conditioned by age but by the superior imperative of nonwithdrawal. And a European, tempted to hilarity, should remember that many of his elemental securities are dependent on the American, childish, stubborn denial of surrender. In a society where achievement is slowly losing its meaning because of the inflation of achievements, this attitude toward life seems to me admirable.

THE COSMIC MISDEMEANOR OF McLUHANISM

Marshall McLuhan turns his penetrating intelligence against intelligence, a grave error as well as a misdemeanor and betrayal. He advocates the limitations of intelligence, thereby jeopardizing mankind's future. His theories are convincing but to proclaim them without considering the eventual losses is extremely dangerous. More than half of the world is already in the hands (if not the lethal grip!) of the quarter-intelligent and semi-literate who, in many countries, claim the right to prescribe morals and legislate consciences. In our part of the planet, the lowbrow is already the legislator of predilection but does not dare dream about conscience. I am afraid that Professor McLuhan facilitates his repulsive career. He assures him that his victory is inevitable. He informs him of his frightful power.

Some Remarks on the Trouble with Violence

We are witnessing a vehement discussion on violence. The American press has begun to ponder whether the meticulous description, naturalism, and systematic portrayal of violence seek to propagandize or have a didactic value. They are quite late, one is tempted to observe.

They point out that in the early movies, we find as much violence as in the contemporary ones, but that no one complained of it and its consequences. They miss the real sense of the phenomenon, but they unconsciously touch the problem's core. Of course, violence *was* present in the movies of William Hart, Buck Jones, Hoot Gibson, Douglas Fairbanks, Ken Maynard, Charlie Chaplin, Rod LaRocque, Walter Brennan, George Bancroft, Wallace Beery, Gary Cooper, James Cagney and Humphrey Bogart, an even more poignant violence in black-and-white than in today's Technicolor-Ketchup rendition. But at the same time, early American cinema, being a fresh, popular, and folksy art, knew by nature and intuition how and where to draw the demarcation line between Good and Evil, how to render Good credible and appealing, and Evil odious and despicable. This socially- and culturally-valuable knowledge (seen by many as vulgar and easy but being in fact very refined and difficult to attain) Hollywood has completely lost; such distinctions have gone astray among all kinds of psychologism, relativism, and pseudorealism. Uncondemned violence is simply antididactic. The Great Art of how to condemn, and how to inspire the audience to condemn, has vanished from today's Hollywood manual of easy truths.

THE NEW PROMISCUOUS LEFT

Revolutions start in the name of virtue and chastity. They are prepared for by years of well-advertised longing for better morals and manners, for a rigidity that is considered behavioral grace. Frivolity is antiprogressive before a revolution and reactionary after it. The ambiguous charms of lust are condemned as sin against the People as well as against the Ideal, despite the fact that the Folk and the Absolute have nothing in common. The evils of voluptuousness, vice, debauchery, prurience, and excess always stand with the enemy of revolution, no matter what his circumstances are—a boorish villager or a depraved aristocrat. To enjoy and exhaust life was always somewhat contradictory to the essence of revolutionary thought and procedure that, in principle, concentrates on the future. Only the decaying and perishing classes have no time and must hurry with their pleasures. Revolutionaries are supposed to have plenty of time; if not, they risk being accused of doubts. The Puritans were the extreme Left of their epoch. Danton and Robespierre personified supersquare purity. Marx, Engels, and Lenin abhorred everything connected with the excesses of flesh. Asceticism has always been the core of revolutionary zeal and the hard steel of its armor.

The honor of destroying this clear and clean set of values, category of ideas, and hierarchy of means fell to that part of the American Left concentrated spiritually around the Berkeley Campus. With engaging innocence, they promote debauchery, with winning self-confidence, they preach theories whose inherent incoherence first amuses a European, then forces him to ponder the monumentality of intellectual chaos. Just how collective copulation will eliminate poverty or broaden and deepen popular culture will probably forever remain a sweet secret of Berkeley militants. Narcotics as an alternative to the ideals of common daily life experienced by mankind and sought for some five thousand years is an outrageously funny notion. But what wipes the smile from one's lips is the question of how and where the Berkeleyans managed to connect childish irresponsibility toward their own lives with revolution, Marxism, radicalism, leftism? Or, more seriously: is the contemporary, subcultural stress on decadence and decay an essential characteristic of social, political, and intellectual leftism? Let's hope, rather, that it is a consequence of a penchant toward primitive intellectual impulses as a substitute for modern humanism.

Decadent subcultures that accept degeneracy as a value and behavioral norm are as old as the world, but they have never disguised themselves as forces of social progress. The perennial mark of decadence is its individualism and lack of social conscience. Moreover, a complete decadent scorns every social and moral engagement. How a Berkeleyan identifies his feelings of responsibility regarding the Vietnam war with his compulsive worship of a limitless sex life remains a mystery to me. The once offbeat stigma of drug addiction is as common with modern hippies as it was to a nineteenth-century dandy, but the latter never wanted to spread the habit, while the former consider it a mission. On the contrary, a dandy jealously guarded his uniqueness and unusual social stance. The nineteenth century in Europe knew the phenomenon of intellectual groups who turned artistry into ideology. They had a strong inclination toward every abuse of morals and manners, toward their refinement and perversion, but they shunned politics. It is difficult to imagine any of their ideologues, from Baudelaire to Oscar Wilde and Aubrey Beardsley, embracing a socialist cause. At the peak of their success and influence in European culture, they felt terribly artistocratic and antiegalitarian, considering themselves a charismatic elite. They spoke of satanism and "Naked Soul" as a Berkeleyan speaks of psychedelic philosophies; they smoked hashish and inhaled ether as Haight–Ashbury indigenes do pot—and with like aims and reasons—but they never considered it a departure point for communal activity. Enough evidence exists to believe that both Wilde and Beardsley (the incontestable father of current psychedelic art) would rather be enamored of fascism and Hitlerism, as many of their Italian and German confrères were, than with any Marxian derivatives. A faithful decadent espoused Nietzsche's gospel of the Better and the Strong, of the hero with the right to abuse because he is ever ready to perish. But this predilection placed a self-respecting decadent far from social commitment— if we're not disposed to equate with social commitment his probable, future, ultimate vocation as an SS man in Auschwitz.

In the beginning of this century, certain radicals and socialists, enthusiastic about scientific progress in the field of new, improved, rubber contraceptives, preached woman's liberation from eternal bondage, having in mind, of course, masculine brutality and economic domination. One of them, George Bernard Shaw (a vegetarian with rather meager sexual experience) went so far as to advocate so-called "sexual freedom." Being a theoretician, Mr. Shaw could easily enjoy fame as a radical, though he was careful to propagandize just a woman's right to choose her love partner and not to sell herself and her body. Still, promiscuity seemed to him a mark of the depraved rich. The following decades saw socialists and Communists of both sexes abundantly sleeping together despite the lack of official Church or State approbation. This led to accusations from more conservative elements but was still far from debauchery. Just the opposite: according to literary testimony, leftish lovers were prone to suicide and other romantic and tragic means, such as killing each other on grounds of unrequited feeling, jealousy, or infidelity. One must admit, it's difficult to imagine a contemporary Berkeleyite commiting suicide because of unrequited love or killing out of jealousy; he would be forced to kill an entire cocktail party plus large circles of friends and remote acquaintances.

The Berkeley cohesion of leftism and promiscuity is, in European eyes, old-fashioned. The attempt to undermine the existing order and to impose a new one by means of multiple sexual effort or intensified drug hallucination sounds like a joke from the era of primitive anarchism. A holy social war in the defense of lesbian delights or the human right to transvestism proves just one thing: that the construction of American society (except in its minority problems) is unbearably healthy and in the best shape. A modern Marxist, despite all Russian and Chinese distortions of the genuine formula, still builds his thinking on the distinction between the base and superstructure. Submerged by the insoluble problems of ideological struggle, political mechanism, and economic planning, he has no time for sin—even if he does not consider excessive lovemaking as a sin. Promiscuity is for him a part of the superstructure; it flourishes only when the base is sound, firm, powerful, well-functioning. For him Berkeley and hippie-dom are painful evidences that the American base is in perfect order, and that only a booming economy could afford an extravaganza like Haight–Ashbury and the love movement. Psychedelic leftism or narcotic socialism make him suspicious that perverse fakes are being mounted by the CIA to convince the world that everything goes well in America and to hide the real trouble. In the eyes of a hard-core French Communist or a Russian party official, the Berkeley fancies are a subversive intrigue, devilishly organized to discredit real progressiveness: hippies are secret service agents and Haight–Ashbury is the Establishment's poison in the soul of American youth longing for authentic social revolt and justice. In Russia, young people who took part in sex parties would have been jailed immediately for counterrevolutionary activity and accused of subverting communism. An adolescent who by some miracle acquires pot and smokes it risks a nice ten-year term in a concentration camp for being an agent of American imperialism and contaminating the happy and healthy Soviet youth.

What remains to be explained is why the first genuine American style of depravity (in both a mental and biological sense) obviously seeks moral decency? This striving is undeniable: every "Take acid!" appeal is accompanied by: ". . . and don't kill little Vietnamese!" A "Long live screwing . . ." slogan has an obligatory annex: ". . . for everybody!"—these last two words providing a muscular touch of social idealism. Freudians might ascribe it to the subconscious at work; the conservatives wouldn't hesitate to call it hypocrisy. For me it is evidence of that glorious, victorious Americanism which lustful leftists from Berkeley want so passionately and hopelessly to be rid of. The European decadent, dandy, degenerate, bohemian, libertine, narcomaniac, Nirvana wanderer, sex maniac, and theoretician of orgiastics would say, as he always did: "*Après nous le déluge. . . .*" His American counterpart still wants to improve the world and distribute the goods, even if the only values to distribute are debauchery, degeneracy, and decay.

DILETTANTISM (2)

To me, these days, dilettantism seems the proudest intellectual attitude. Too much systematized and fanatically-enforced knowledge leads to all kinds of ugly relativism. Dilettantism means impartiality. If only its judgments are mature, it may equal the wisdom of the ancients. It is the sole escape from successful stupidity disguised as innovation and progress. Together with the insane accumulation of codified science that tends to elude any human control, dilettantism becomes more and more a position of intellectual dignity. Isn't it more honorable *not* to know for sure than to know too much and too well? Those who have survived Hitler and Stalin feel a sort of coherent, though inexplicable, certitude about this.

WISDOM? WHAT'S THAT?

A recently elected president of the National Student Association, who has reached the awe-inspiring age of 23 years, declared to the press: "We're going to turn this damned country around. We're going to make it stand up and do the right thing!"

It remains obscure, however, how this gentleman knows what the right thing is. Countless philosophers, statesmen, and social thinkers have died not knowing it. Many who still live, if honest enough, admit that they too are not certain. I presume I'm not incorrect if I assume that they might know more about many things than this young man, unless we attribute to him a supernatural force of intuition. However, less knowledge may be better knowledge—Jean Jacques Rousseau, at least, believed so. But Hitler and Stalin did as well. Lenin wrote that he tried to construct a state that every cook could run. It opened new horizons for the entire culinary profession, but fifty years later, the results have proved rather doleful.

GAMES INTELLECTUALS PLAY

I was taken to dinner by a prosperous New York intellectual with very leftish opinions. The New Left intellectual, he argued at the table, has the freedom to oppose only because he has little influence on the masses and so is powerless. On the other hand, the Russian or Eastern European intellectual is deprived of that freedom because he is powerful within the society. My host thus eliminated *a priori* those principles, moral or ideological, that distinguish the American political and social structure from the Russian–Communist. Apparently it comforted him in a somewhat masochistic way.

Strangely enough, he stubbornly refused to recognize that the influence of the intellectual in opposition in Communist Europe comes from the ideas he preaches and fights for, and not just because he is an intellectual. Never has the writer been hailed because he writes but for *what* he writes. An anti-Communist Eastern European intellectual has power because he opposes a more powerful power, one that uses its might to oppress, subjugate, and harm entire nations and countries. His strength derives from his persecution, his righteousness. He is in empathy with his society and is ready to pay with his personal freedom. His influence therefore springs mainly from his anti-communism. The faithful Communist intellectual who is out of sympathy with the masses—and there are plenty—is, in a Communist-ruled country, as impotent as the complaining leftist in America. *Il y a quelque chose là-dedans. . . .*

I sympathized with my host. "All you need," I said as we sipped our after-dinner Rémy-Martin, "is to be a little oppressed. A nice, cozy, but not too harmful, persecution would do."

Yet, it remained a disturbing matter: who could, if

need be, oppress him? I understood the futility of my advice: after all, the American intellectual tries hard and all in vain! It is, generally, the impossibility of being persecuted that is the source of frustration. Of course, he *thinks* of himself as one that *is* oppressed. But by whom? I desperately looked around for an oppressor to comfort him—and I was unable to find one.

ESSENTIAL OMISSION

The Western world disposes of fairly accurate and exhaustive knowledge of Communist crimes against, and persecution of, human beings. What it doesn't know is what communism makes of a man *without* persecution. This could be the main reason for many of the West's defeats when dealing with communism.

HOW SIMPLE!

The dedicated in advertising and at the universities try to find a formula to express America's fabulous wealth, both for propaganda purposes and for their personal contentment. I think it should be expressed by the relation between the plenitude of food and the widespread, almost social, refusal to eat. In the eyes of a citizen of a Communist country, the diet obsession is an absurd, insolent whim. But only the rich can afford not to eat and to live on something else. The poor haven't even an idea of what it might be.

THE INTELLECTUAL'S FALLACIOUS GLORIES

It is generally accepted that our epoch has seen the triumph of the intellectual. In my opinion, the opposite is true. A successful intellectual is a contradiction of nature, as mankind for centuries has held unsuccessful, embittered, skeptical, and disappointed sages in higher

esteem than the joyful and self-contented ones. The combination of brain skills, bitterness, and lack of success
give to the intellectual two precious traits: exceptionality
and dignity. Without them, he would become ludicrous.
An intellectual's destiny bears something both doleful
and humorous, exhilarating and lamentable, comic and
pitiful; charm is the one ingredient that can save him
from inevitable humiliation. Socrates, the charming proto-
type of the intellectual, notwithstanding his frequent
failures, never lost dignity in men's eyes. Hence, his
superiority over Sartre who, being wealthy and apparently
successful, can claim neither charm nor dignity because of his obsequiousness to the most dubious causes
doggedly labeled as "progressive." The demographic explosion of intellectuals, characteristic of our time, robs
them of a priceless feature: rareness. The present social
scene is replete with updated Tristram Shandys, pocket-
size Voltaires, mass-produced Julien Sorels, countlessly
reprinted Stephen Dedaluses. The sovereignty of personal
opinion and originality of thought gets lost in the crowds.
One hundred years ago, the disillusioned victim of unfulfilled dreams or of unrealized ideas was thought interesting; he could enchant parties and stir rapt admiration. He was the product of a lack of comprehension and
legitimate, if mistreated, ambitions. Today, when *les
bourgeois* happily discuss the farthest-out topics at the
breakfast table and are eager to share in the most off-beat
concepts or to participate in the wildest moral adventures,
the impoverished, unsuccessful intellectual is merely sad
and miserable. He possesses nothing to compel respect. All
that is left for him is to extend his youthfulness endlessly,
following the latest fashions, pretending to be vigorous
at parties where he sports both silver hair and childish
amulets or beads, and dances farcically, hoping that his
exhibitionism will pass for eccentricity.

SOME REMARKS ON THE NATURE OF
REBELLION IN COMMUNISM

In Communist-ruled societies, the facts are opaque.
They cannot be defined and verified as in a democracy.
Interpretations might come closer to the truth than actual
empirical findings. A moral evaluation can be made by
examining functions or remote results.

When dealing with today's communism, Western scientists and observers tend to ascribe changes mainly to dis-
sents within the party. They believe in heresies, schisms,
and the corrosive role of culture. The erosion of the ideology within the political framework of power seems to them
the most decisive and progressive factor. This element is
of crucial significance—and they are right in emphasizing
it—but the tendency to overlook other factors of change,
to underestimate or abandon them, is a basic mistake.
Changes result from the monumental passive resistance
of the oppressed societies, a source of gigantic economic
and social failure of communism. The disenchanted
Stalinists do not produce changes, but the inevitable
necessity of change produces disenchanted Stalinists.
Polish or Hungarian intellectuals did not originate revolt.
The pressure of social facts forced them to recognize the
irrevocability of upheaval. The famous flamboyant mani-
festos of Polish and Hungarian poets, praised in the West
as magnificent sparks of rebellion, are totally forgotten
today; but the stress of anti-communism deep in the
masses ruled by Communists is overwhelmingly present
and will never cease to exist. The poets do not create
changes. They hitch on to them.

The case of the Soviet poet Yevtushenko may throw
some light on that common miscomprehension. It's easy
to understand why Yevtushenko is called a "rebel" by the
Soviet government, but why the Western press does the

same remains incomprehensible to everyone behind the Iron Curtain. When young, he was unquestionably an admirer of Stalin, who was then in power. Admirers of Yevtushenko call this youthful error and acclaim his conversion to anti-Stalinism as a mark of poetic grandeur. They do not remark, or easily ignore, that he became an anti-Stalinist when no danger threatened and all the glory was reserved for the anti-Stalinists. He then was a supporter of Khrushchev, who had the means to protect and reward his supporters, even if they were slightly disobedient. Since the fall of Khrushchev, Yevtushenko has not defended his fallen Maecenas. He considered himself an independent Leninist, which was exactly what the new administration of Brezhnev and Kosygin expected from its poets.

Western man's ethos is built on the rational and voluntary recognition of evil, a constant distinction between the bad and the good, and the perennial quest for the true and the just. From such attitudes, his universal morality and personal dignity derive. He finds it rather tasteless should someone noisily trample a defeated evil without having taken part in the previous struggle, without having been willing to pay with his own security or act with courage in the moment of peril. Such behavior is often branded as cowardice by Western standards. It is then more mysterious that Yevtushenko is rewarded the title of "rebel" for just condemning but not fighting. Attacking Stalinism in a time when such attacks meant no more than polemics, invited no more than threats in print from hard-core dogmatists, and did not involve any personal losses may in no way be called rebellion. Rebellion is an attempt to overthrow a strongly-protected order or sacrosanct values despite personal jeopardy. Russia is filled with people who fit this definition. But Yevtushenko is not one of them. A rebel is hardly one who is constantly rewarded by those against whom he is "revolting." Yevtushenko, strangely enough, obtains the most lavish privileges from his country's Establishment, that which he pretends to criticize and challenge.

Some Western observers and scholars admit that their indulgence for Yevtushenko is stimulated by his position and role in Soviet ideological splits and the game of factions. Having to choose between Ilychev and Kochetov on one side and Yevtushenko and Tvardovsky on the other, we obviously prefer the latter men. Yevtushenko is an overt, even if circumstantial, anti-Stalinist, currently involved with the more approachable camp. His anti-reactionary zeal is beyond any doubt. But the post-Stalinist developments in Russia do not necessarily mean a clear shifting toward values we in the West consider fundamental and irreversible. We need only observe how Polish and Hungarian anti-Stalinism, after being assured the power, turned into a more complex and sophisticated tyranny, annihilating values it claimed to defend, hiding behind a perversely-constructed mask of progressivity. This anti-Stalinism constitutes an even hardier and more impenetrable menace than primitively diabolic Stalinism. Yevtushenko's position in Sinyavski's trial, his lies and cynical remolding of truth, are clues to how the new anti-Stalinism may operate. His vulgar careerism disguised as spiritual independence is another, and the blundering in the West in evaluating the picture is a third. One who has not lived in a Communist society is incapable of grasping where the gimmick and the hoax lie, or why Yevtushenko is so hated there by all the more worthy, the honest, and the helpless.

A HANG-UP

"*It is our duty* to protest!" my host said.

We sat in a charming Village apartment, its atmosphere and décor so tasteful that I wouldn't have protested even if I had been held there by force for a couple of years.

"Your *duty*?" I repeated, lost in meditation.

"What's wrong with that word?" he asked suspiciously.

"I suppose it's rather a lucrative occupation today. Especially to protest against an actual, authentic freedom. It is a new industry, a new way of making money, and accumulating affluence. Three things are necessary to start this kind of business: a pen, a guitar, and a free society as one's professional space. Written protests bring decent livings, vocal protests bring millions. One who knows how effectively to exhibit his social misery and anguish rapidly becomes a millionaire. The *how* is very important; the expression of misery and anguish must be skilfully directed. Many of the protesters do not stop midway; not only do they protest against the existing actual freedom; they praise, limitlessly, what they call *genuine* freedom, which they say is found east of the Iron Curtain. They call themselves cautious Communists. Now, to be a cautious Communist is even more lucrative than to be a protester. The cautious Communists flourish chiefly in France and Italy, where the radical feelings of the masses are very distinct. There they call themselves protesters against the social order that gives them a *dolce vita* the United States protesters can not even dream about. Several cautious French or Italian Communist writers, painters, and film directors have collected sums of wealth that might make the average United States tycoon embittered. As Communists, they are cautious because they are careful to avoid living in those societies that have already realized the social justice that they preach and recommend in their works of art. They consider living under social injustice more reasonable. I suspect that they couldn't live without it. Curiously enough, in the Communist countries, there are also plenty of cautious Communist writers, painters, and film directors. They are extremely careful to avoid the slightest remark about social injustice in their societies, and they glorify, cautiously, their Communist social order and government; if they did so in a reckless way, those around them would hold them for idiots, which they cannot afford for purely professional reasons. In such societies, there are also a number of protesters, but they are in prison or in a state of starvation, because they cannot publish, make movies, or sing songs . . ."

I noticed that my monologue tended to be confusing and much too long indeed. Perhaps for that reason, I have never received another invitation to the charming Village apartment.

MUSING ON CHANGE

I met a scholar who said he believes that communism is the only force able to change the world. "Interesting," I admitted, "but then why doesn't it begin with itself? Why doesn't it change into something better? Why are the Communists who want to change communism usually in prison?" And I added: "Perhaps, because it is easier to change the world than the habit of using prisons . . ."

He looked at me with distaste, probably thinking: "Why are people so petty? Why are they concerned with the tiny problems of penitentiary systems when the world's fate is at stake?"

THE TRAPS OF PREORDAINED THINKING

At American universities here and there, I run into names and types familiar from my Eastern European past. I remember them as ardent Stalinists whose principal preoccupation was vilifying America. As faithful, orthodox, thoroughly-trained Marxist-Communists, they were preaching in word and print America's moral, political, socioeconomic monstrosity and failure; its uttermost inferiority compared with the Soviet Union; its antihuman intentions, and poisonous influence. The spreading of anti-American venom was their vocation. I suppose many of their readers and disciples who now live in Eastern Europe are still infected with their dialectically-refined and intellectually well-shaped hatred. But then, fortune's wheel turned, Stalinism was defeated at least for the time being, and devoted Stalinists had either to repent, atone and become very modest, or else leave. Many have left. Some of them I uncover now on American campuses, preaching and analyzing the Soviet Union's and communism's defects, claiming that they never ceased being faithful Marxists, discreetly advocating some changes in their home of refuge. I do not wonder excessively, for life teaches us that the one slandered often turns out to be the only rescue. Yet I can't imagine a Birchite, fearing difficulties in America, looking for shelter in Russia, finding is, and being invited to lecture at Moscow University.

Peace March in New York

I felt sad looking at her. How much, and how well, I know about this kind of young Jewish girl, her eyes filled with the hatred of evil (this time code signal: LBJ), and with purest ideological intentions. Little girls with unclean nails who, in the end, are always poor victims of their own: "I know better *how* it *really* is . . ." Today they pin psychedelic Marxian buttons on their busts and carry posters on which Ho Chi Minh smiles with tactful malice, for he knows how it really is. Thirty years ago, they marched through the streets of Eastern European cities with little photos of Joseph Stalin where now they exhibit the serene motto "Make love not war." An impressive number of them perished, just a few years later, in the most abominable, verminous concentration camps scattered over Kazakhstan and Siberia by their mustachioed idol. What Jehovah might do for their New York sisters is to allow them to protest perennially, and be wrong and unwashed just as a sign of dissent, not of human degradation.

THE ELUSIONS AND TRAPS OF INNOCENCE, ANNO 1967

We sat among trees, the serenity of a Connecticut landscape around us. One of the ladies, a devoted reader of mass circulation magazines, said: "How good it is that, finally, she can find her peace here, this poor, gentle woman . . ."

"She has auburn hair," another lady added.

"And she is so charming," another said. "As innocent as she is . . ."

"What makes you use this adjective?" I asked.

"She hasn't ever had a bank account. I read it in a magazine."

"Individuals in Soviet Russia do not own bank accounts," I said. "Institutions do. Some versatile sycophants who produce propaganda movies and songs are forced to put their excess of earned money in special savings accounts; but, according to Communist mores, it would not be *comme-il-faut* if a top political leader or his family even had a savings account. The lack of one is hardly a proof of innocence."

"You don't like her?" one of the ladies asked.

"Anyway, I do not believe in collective responsibility," I answered warily.

"But what should she be responsible for?" exclaimed the first lady. "She cannot be judged for her father's sins, for heaven's sake!"

"Of course not. But she can and must be evaluated for her approach to her father's sins."

"She was a daughter," a lady declared solemnly. "Do you know what that means? How do you dare expect a daughter to totally condemn her own father. One has to be a daughter oneself to grasp her anguish. You . . . ," the lady looked at me with antipathy, ". . . have never been a daughter, and you're unable to understand her."

"Your point is correct, Madam," I said. "Being a daughter, she was incapable, by nature, of worthwhile testimony. But she *was* able to avoid the glaring distortions of truth and embarrassing superficiality that characterize her book. She witnessed, from a close distance, one of the most horrible monsters mankind has ever known. However, all we get from her is a picture of a boorish, not too bright, bully who died in an abject, repulsive way. And where is the genius of evil, the author of the most perverse mass-slaughter in history? Who was more destined than she to give better evidence of the demonic balance between the bloody, primitive violence of his instincts and the bottomless perfidies of his mind?"

"She was his daughter . . ." one lady said, a little weaker.

"He was one of the two greatest political criminals of this century. The population of a huge part of the world once ruled by him will remember that forever. Many historians see him, and with good reason, as a more disastrous threat to humanity than Hitler. Base, ignominious, and innumerable crimes were committed by him or in his name; the amount of human suffering, both in the physical and in the spiritual sense, that he inflicted absolutely equals what Hitler did. His name has been cursed with stiffening lips by millions of murdered beings whose only reason for death was his will. For the other millions, between the Pacific and the Elbe, his name was tantamount to those of Nero, Attila, Genghis Khan, Ivan the Terrible, or, more simply, Satan or Antichrist—and loathed like disease. He was devilishly ugly, repulsive, with the specific ugliness of soul and body that comes with cruelty, hatred, hypocrisy, and treachery. Specially trained artists tried constantly to touch-up and change his photographs to implant in his physiognomy the tiniest trace of that goodness so indispensable to the official portraits of rulers; they never succeeded in extracting from his eyes that brutal stare, the uncontrolled bestiality, and endless contempt for others that made him the most ruthless murderer of his own closest associates in the history of modern politics. However, no notion of any of this was contained in her report."

"She was his daughter. . . ." sighed a lady helplessly.

"Perhaps those who initiated the affair," I said, "should have foreseen that."

"Are you suggesting," a gentleman said, "that the entire operation of bringing and sheltering her in this country may be an error?"

"No," I denied firmly. "If someone asks for political asylum, the moral duty and *raison d'être* of a free society is to grant it. Besides, the Russian revolution had four great leaders: Lenin, Dzerzhinsky, Trotsky, and Stalin. Lenin was childless. Trotsky's son finished his life in the West. Dzerzhinski's family lives in London. Stalin's daughter is in America. It's comforting for those who do not appreciate the Russian revolution."

"I believe in political pragmatism," another gentleman said "and in the light of what you just said, we Americans made a good deal. In terms of propaganda of course."

"I'm not so sure," I said. "The results are still relative and ambiguous. The sole beneficiary, so far, seems to be the American press and the publishing industry whose uninhibited, grotesque publicity and allegations probably kept her blushing; the orgy of irresponsible comparisons of her writing with that of Turgenev and Pasternak have shamed anyone with literary taste. The real trouble, however, lies with the American underestimate of the element of insult, especially when dealing with Russian, or Eastern European, moral supersensitivity. For people there the word "Stalin" equals utmost evil; emperors who crucify their nations leave their self-earned hate as the hideous legacy of their progeny, even if the latter are the sweetest persons under the sun. No matter how poignantly and sincerely Stalin's daughter mourns her childhood's and adolescence's tragic exceptionality, "privilege" has always been the key word to her fate. And privilege is her destiny in this country, at least in the eyes of her father's former subjects—the three million dollars collected in royalties make them think immediately of the thirty million imprisoned, tortured, killed, and perished during Stalin's rule in the concentration camps of Siberia and Kazakhstan. They cannot help thinking it inhuman that the weight of human corpses and blood makes the fee heavier, and the price of a memoir increases madly according to the amount of wrong done by one of its protagonists. We can take it for granted that the memoirs of any other daughter of any other contemporary statesman, ruler, or tyrant could never achieve that level of financial reward. The logical conclusion drawn by a Russian might therefore be as simple as this: while in Russia the combat against the ghost of Stalinism is the most crucial matter of life and death, America rescues and harbors its remnants. Two reporters in a New York monthly gave a detailed, factual account of her case, pointing out the suspicious, enigmatic smoothness with which she escaped from under the tutelage of the Soviet Embassy in New Delhi. I wouldn't wonder if twenty years from now we'll find some files indicating that her sensational flight westward was watched with enigmatic benevolence by some obscure agency in the very womb of the KGB . . ."

There was a moment of silence. "Well," said one of the gentlemen, "that could possibly be the worst."

"No," I said. "The worst is implicit in her book. From her position as daughter, granddaughter, niece, cousin, relative, and friend, she recreated a certain reality in a

77 · *From the Notebook of a Dilettante*

most false, distorted way. Her family, through the fallacious magic of personal treatment, becomes an innocent,
noble group of individuals caught in the nightmarish
gears of history, ravaged by mysterious misfortunes,
plagues, winds of destiny, and undeserved harms. The
truth was different. Her family represented a historical
archetype of our epoch's political banditry, and each of
its members had his hands stained with the blood of
murdered Russians, Georgians, Armenians, and Ukrain-
ians whose only guilt was that of being non-Communist,
non-Bolshevik, or insubmissive enough during the family's
rise to power. She complains bitterly in her book that
Beria's villainy made them disappear one after another,
but she doesn't offer one word to all those slaughtered and
annihilated by *them*. I can hardly feel any sympathy with
her beloved uncles and cousins so warmly described, nor
feel sorry for their violent deaths in the dungeons of the
dirtiest secret police in mankind's chronicles, which they
created themselves. I do not find the defeat of Communist bigotry and its mindless fanaticism sympathetic.
I am not moved by the pseudotragedies of the betrayed
henchmen and devoted coauthors of a most savage system of random mass extinction used to terrorize and
subjugate, a system that finally destroyed them, its con-
structors."

"But those people were good to her . . ." a lady sighed.
"One is always, in a sense, a victim of one's own equivocal
reality . . ."

"This is true," I said. "They were good to her. Their
chastity, in her vision, derived from the fact that they
were human and loyal to each other and did not murder
their fellow-Communists. But she never asked them about
the other thing they did. She gives them all too easy
absolution. Millions of readers of her book will do the
same. This is the cornerstone of the abuse. It might be

that some really innocent, naive housewife in Ohio or Colorado will close that volume with: 'Oh, what a poor girl. She had such an *insupportable* father.' "

REVENGE

After being saved, rescued, fed, and restored as a national entity and social body by America twice during this century, the French behave in a most ungrateful way, exhibiting towards their benefactors ingratitude at its worst. This mean aversion results in an open hatred quite comprehensible in the light of timeless human relations between a generous, powerful spender and a petty, jealous receiver. But lately the French have exceeded their infatuation and aroused disgust even in the indulgent Americans. The latter speak about retaliation but as usual commit an error by wrongly evaluating the other's sensitivity. The French, regardless of their magnificent cultural heritage, are extremely callous as a nation; allusion does not reach them. They are perceptive only of their own grand gestures and grandiloquence but rarely bother with the dignity of others. Thus, the suggestion of bringing back the ashes of American soldiers fallen in France's defense won't impress them. Tact and delicacy is no longer considered a virtue, unless their own profit is involved. The only way to punish them and bring them back to decency of manners is to deprive them of something they consider a necessity—Paris, for example. America's power of reproduction is limitless, and I believe it would be child's play to create a new Paris through contemporary American technology and perfectionism. It should be recreated somewhere in Venezuela or Uruguay as it is better not to deprive the Americans of using their passports when they go to Paris. Such a new Paris could easily contain all the charms of the old—the ancient churches and caves, her romantic moods, flower vendors, sentimentally crooked streets, *croissants* and *valse-java*—just fabricated and canned. It would be easy to find enough traitors among the French who, for good American dollars, will bring over all the most sacrosanct French secrets, be it about the cuisine, the wine, or cruel ways of extorting money from tourists. It will smell a little of Disneyland, but then who says that it is impossible to enjoy Disneyland?

ICE HOCKEY AND DIALECTIC

This year, we celebrate half a century of practical communism in Russia. It has succeeded in creating a social reality close to an absolute evil. It is responsible for jailing and murdering millions of innocent people, subjugating millions more to misery and deterioration, and robbing other millions of their right to personal endeavor and progress—perhaps the most precious element of human existence. Strangely enough, after such a record, communism never stops pretending that it is mankind's only path to absolute perfection. Meanwhile democracy, communism's opposite in the contemporary world, is nonsensically and obsessively convinced of its own innumerable evils. Yet man has invented nothing better than a soundly-functioning democracy, be it in ancient Athens, contemporary Copenhagen, or Gary, Indiana. Those who live under communism are fully aware of that.

The situation is in a sense similar to that which exists in the realm of ice hockey. Every two years, the World Ice Hockey Amateur League sponsors an international ice hockey contest. The democracies send amateur players, and the Communists send professionals disguised as amateurs. The helplessness exhibited by the international jury in accepting professionals as amateurs is the result of the Communists' power of argumentation. They persuade them that when a player doesn't receive money— just apartments, clothes, food, half a year's free vacations in the most expensive seaside resorts, television sets for every game, and expensive extra presents for each marked point—he is not a professional but an amateur. Of course, these Communist amateur teams steal easy victories from democratic team players who purchase even their hockey sticks with their own money. The victories are presented in the Communist press all over the world as proof of communism's superiority over degenerating capitalism, never mentioning, naturally, that in capitalism, professional ice hockey teams exist that could with little effort smash each Communist team to pieces. In democracies, no one cares, but in Communist-dominated societies the masses, being too tired to pursue the truth, passively agree with the headline which proclaims new victories of the invincible red, Communist, people's ice hockey *amateur* team.

Such total havoc regarding the social consciences of the two sides makes communication impossible.

THE LIE AND POLITICS

Delicacy is a common cause of the lie. The relentless pressures of one's sensitivity breeds more liars than any other psychological circumstance. This simple truth applies to everyone—except politicians. No matter what they do for the sake of subtlety, it turns into callousness and fraud.

OTHER DIFFICULTIES WITH DELICACY

Generosity without delicacy is a half-virtue. This is easy to detect in private relations. It is more difficult to operate with delicacy in political and public matters, where awkward generosity might be considered corruption or brutal pressure.

NATIONALISM

For many years, American Kremlinologists have believed that nationalism is the chief erosion force in the

Communist empire. Those of us who came from *over there* tried to persuade them that they were wrong, except for some sly and perfidious Marxists, disguised as progressive revisionists, who—in order to perplex the West—confirmed them in their fallacy. But nationalism, or national communism—as American Kremlinologists used to call it—has proved itself a nipple, a pacifier, in Communist hands. During the Spanish Civil War, Communists demonstrated how perfectly well they use nationalism for their own ends; then, the submission of Eastern Europe after Yalta was carried out with the same nationalistic accompaniment. The newest brand of national communism degenerates easily into populistic jingoism, anti-Semitism, and all kinds of the most vulgar, anti-Russian idiosyncrasies without really harming Communists. Nationalism breeds emotions, but feelings are hardly a menace to any empire. What the Communists are really afraid of are ideas, not emotions; penetrating, analytical thought, not lowbrow patriotism. *Habeas Corpus*, Declaration of Human Rights, and the American Constitution are the concrete enemies, not flags, not anthems, not emblems, not the colors and monuments of Middle-Ages national heroes who are dead long enough to be helpless when they are enlisted as Communist party members in official history textbooks. Rumania may pull faces at the Soviet Union in the most insulting, nationalistic way—it will hardly trigger any invasion because Rumanian internal order is still based on rigid Communist order; Rumanians are permitted to chant patriotic songs, but not to express any doubts about the heart of the matter. The Polish archnationalist a decade ago, Mr. Gomulka, became the staunchest Russian supporter, which doesn't hinder him from using the most jingoistic arguments at home, especially when dealing with Jews. Czechoslovakia, during its eight-month-long, heroic quest for freedom, didn't use any pseudo-patriotic, anti-Russian slogans. It just wanted to think freely, and draw its own conclusions from its own experiences in order to improve its fate—meaning the socialist reality—and this modest demand had to be suppressed by the Russians by force. The only element that endangers the *raison d'état* of the empire is freedom of thought. The empire's erosion will come by means of thinking, not by feeling pride in being a Pole, a Hungarian, or a Bulgarian.

WHERE HAVE ALL THE FLOWERS GONE?

"*But they cannot arrest* a whole nation that doesn't want them in its country!" exclaimed a young, attractive Manhattan girl. "Everyone is against them, and they can't arrest everyone!"

We walked down Second Avenue; pubs, bars, and side-walk coffee houses were filled with her mini-skirted, paisley-covered, pajama-trousered sisters. It was a warm, gregarious, New-York-in-the-East-Sixties evening, the fourth in a row of the most cynical violence staged by one nation against another during the last twenty years and called, officially, the Czech crisis. News just reached us that the Russians intended a mass arrest of all Czechs suspected of being liberal-minded or, at least, reluctant about the Russian invasion and occupation of their country.

"Why not," I said. "Of course they can. We've seen events like that in Europe, especially in Russia."

"But . . . ," she smiled incredulously, "suppose they do arrest them? What do they do with them? Who's going to watch such a mass of people? How will they be fed?"

"Small worry. Feeding is no problem where political prisoners are concerned. They are expected to starve. The proletariat works hard and is not obliged to feed its foes, even if they are its members. Russia is a very congenial country for such undertakings; its gigantic, deadly emptiness allows perfect discretion. In the thirties, Russians exterminated some four million Ukrainian peasants who opposed agricultural collectivization. No one even knows where their collective graves are. After the last war the entire ethnic minority of Crimean Tartars and nearly half of the population of Lithuania—some three million people altogether—were subjected to the same treatment on grounds of their alleged hostility towards the Soviet Union's principles. A few million Czechs and Slovaks won't make much trouble for experienced specialists."

"You're infatuated with your hatred of the Soviets, and you can't be trusted . . . ," she was apparently vexed. "No normal person would believe that!"

"I know," I said melancholically. "It's much handier to believe that the marines kill little children in Vietnam."

"This we can see with our own eyes on every TV news program," she said triumphantly.

"Certainly, you're right," I sighed with more melancholy. "I'm always overlooking the American access to so-called free information."

"And who could execute an operation arresting several million people?" she asked, bitingly. "Russian soldiers? Why, soldiers do not arrest people just because they do not like them very much."

"American soldiers don't. But Russians have other manners. During the first day of their invasion, the Slovaks in Bratislava bombed Soviet tanks with paper balls. I found it groovy, indeed, a remarkable manifestation of ingenuity, peaceful intentions, and well-marked rejection as well. The Russian soldiers didn't share the same sense of humor: they fired into the crowd and killed many. But I doubt they would be burdened with arresting balky Czechoslovaks—they came to liberate them from eventual imperialist subjugation, as the formal Soviet statement worded it, so it would somehow be inconsistent to arrest them. The task will be turned over to the KGB which, I can assure you, will perform a flawless job. You know what the KGB is?"

"Of course," she said proudly. "The Russian CIA."

"Not exactly. There are significant differences between the two institutions."

"Differences?" She resorted to open mockery. "Might you, perhaps, point them out to me?"

"Easily. I don't know how many people work for the CIA, but according to official Soviet statistics there are two million special KGB troops, and seemingly a corresponding number of civilian employees, which amounts to nearly three percent of the entire Soviet population. There are whole towns populated exclusively by KGB members and their families, whole branches of industry producing, for example, electronic equipment for bugging, that are restricted to the KGB's control. A network of prisons and concentration camps exists, exclusively under KGB's sway and supervision, which no regular Russian may look into, let alone intervene in. KGB members have a much higher standard of living than the rest of the population; they have their own shops where they get better goods for less money than the average citizen, and they have their private, luxurious seaside resorts that a man from the street is forbidden to enter. They are uniformed; they can arrest anyone without giving any reason and hold him in detention many years without a trial. They can shoot people without facing the consequences for causing death and injury. Insulting a KGB man, on the other hand, is considered a crime against the state, and punching him in the nose during street unrest results in the death penalty. Can you imagine someone in America sentenced to death because he kicked a CIA man in the bottom? Or imprisoned because he insulted the institution? The majority of United States universities would have to hold their classes in jail, not to mention the ex-cruciating hilarity caused by the idea of an exclusive CIA department store. Hence, for the KGB taking care of and disposing of a few million Czechoslovaks destined to disappear would be child's play."

She walked, silent, for a while. Then she said: "Then why don't we protest? As loud as possible . . ."

"That's what I want to ask you as a representative of American youth and a loquacious speaker for the so-called American political conscience. Where are the huge crowds of protest marchers against injustice and inhumanity that so eagerly burn the American flag? Where are all the valiant, bearded oppression fighters? Where are the ebul-lient Brooklyn writers and the Upper Manhattan novelists? Where are the sensitive-to-every-suffering Chelsea play-wrights, the distinguished, but social-minded Boston poets, the fierce pacifist-pornographers, and the well-born, radical clergymen? Where have all the flowers of the brilliant antiwar demonstrations gone? Where, these days, is the praised, combative, shining spirit of the American intellectual, and where is his sense of social morality?"

A DETROIT PARABLE

Once in Detroit, I met a sedate gentleman who happened to practice the profession of guide. After an initial exchange of opinions, he told a story that I rate among the most important comments on the contempo-rary scene, with an insight into *le mal du siècle* that bears the mark of a great metaphor.

"One day, not long ago," began my companion, "I was summoned to guide a sightseeing tour. I entered the bus and found it filled with Russians, a group of Soviet en-gineers. I was to take them to Ford's River Rouge plant. They were gregarious people, hearty and talkative, and soon a warm atmosphere of simple friendliness was established. We were approaching the plant, and had passed the huge parking lot filled with cars, when I noticed a wave of excitement: they talked, argued and gestured more loudly and vigorously than before. The one who spoke the best English addressed me with a smile: 'Do they prepare themselves like this to impress all their visitors? Or is it just for us?'

" 'What do you mean?' I asked.

" 'The impressive number of cars. It's a flattering illustration of Ford's capacity for production.'

" 'I would have guessed,' I answered, 'that you had already noticed that we possess quite a number of cars in this country. Besides, when you get closer you'll realize most of these are used and old. I doubt if Ford would arrange a display of such cars.'

" 'Then to whom do they belong?'

" 'To the people who work at the plant and in the offices. Workers.'

"The Russian grinned with irony. 'You're kidding,' he said, 'so many cars?'

" 'Listen,' I said, 'I don't know exactly how many of Ford's employees own cars but we won't be much in error if we assume that every second one does.'

" 'That,' said the Russian gravely, 'is typical propaganda stuff.'

"I felt we were standing in two different boats, rapidly drifting apart. 'Look,' I said, 'it's easy to check. You ask the first worker in the assembly line whether he owns a car; he'll tell you.'

"The Russian made a sadly cunning grimace. 'Of course, he will,' he said. 'We know that old trick. The plant is well prepared for our visit. Every worker has learned by heart how to answer our questions. Unless he wants to be fired or arrested he'll have to give the proper answer.'

"I felt overcome with desperate anger. 'O.K.,' I said. 'If

you wish, I'll wait with you on the parking lot until the workday is over. You approach people the moment they unlock their cars, and ask them.'

"The Russian looked amused, as if playing with a child. 'What do you take me for?' he asked, 'an idiot? It's simple to stage such a show. I don't hold Americans for bunglers. If you do something, you do it well. You are a big nation, and you know how to deal with other nations.'

"We reached a dead end. I felt helpless—and disgusted. I could not fathom the impossibility of explaining the obvious to another man, nor understand his denial of the bare truth, but I didn't feel like giving further explanation. Any effort appeared futile. But at the same time, a totally senseless notion came to my mind: maybe he *is* right? The nonsense of such a thought seemed absolute and undeniable, yet I could not help thinking it. Why did he speak in such an assured tone? Perhaps *he* knows something *I* don't? Does he have proof that I'm unaware of? I had the stupidest suspicion based on a nonexistent premise, devoid of any roots in the reality I had known for so many years. 'Look,' I said weakly, 'we have plenty of sight-seeing tours each day. Ford has no time to organize silly happenings for every occasion. They have to work and produce. What makes you think they would waste so much energy preparing for your arrival?'

" 'My friend,' said the Russian solemnly, 'Ford is the pride of America. A nation's pride is a serious matter. We don't blame you for anything when a state's pride is at stake. But please don't take us for fools . . .'

"The other Russians nodded earnestly with comprehension and in total agreement."

Homage to Czechoslovakia

The history of Czech culture centers upon the ambivalence between Jan Hus—the fiery Christian reformer, hero of the Great Schism, burnt at the stake by

the Council of Constance in the fifteenth century, antici-
pating the thought of Calvin and Luther by a hundred
years—and the Good Soldier Schweik—a literary creation
of the great writer Jaroslav Hasek, the astute simpleton
who keeps human decency alive through historical cata-
clysms. Nor should we forget that the Carolinian University of Prague is amongst the oldest in the world, that
Prague was the home of the splendid old Jewish myth
of the Golem, that Franz Kafka was born, lived, and loved
in Prague, that the brilliant satirical writer Karel Capek
was a Czech, that the Czechs started making automobiles
and movies at about the same time as Frenchmen and
Germans, that Thomas Masaryk and Edward Benes were
among the most respected statesmen of Europe between
the wars, and that parliamentary democracy had func-
tioned in Czechoslovakia for twenty years. Resistance was
unavoidable. It started with a debate among writers,
joined later by students with economists also playing an
important part. After four months of strife, the barriers
of the most sacred Communist taboos tumbled down. A
Communist administration in which the personnel of the
censorship office demands its abolition sounds like a fairy
tale about good Communists. Some Czech Communists
were reported to be considering a basic doctrinal reform,
assigning to the Party a new role in the State—one of
leadership, but *not* dominant in *all* aspects of thought
and life.

What has happened in Czechoslovakia, from the first
months of the attempted reform to today's grim obfusca-
tion of its sociopolitical existence, transcends any prior
Eastern European effort to transform the reality imposed
after the last war. Russian reaction to it proves this above
all. But the Czech chapter is not yet closed, and it would
be unwise at this point to express any opinion about what
will happen next or to try to evaluate the impact thus

far. In their literature of the last sixty years, the Czechs have given an analysis of human fright, and of meekness in the face of brutal force, that is close to perfection. They explored the possibilities of fighting oppression with a docile, ironic smile. Perhaps this spiritual quality, identified and described by their writers, best explains their behavior during the trials that have made them the incontestable heroes of the postwar Eastern Europe. In the not too distant future, we will know whether the boldness and sacrifice of their attempt will have resulted in the ideological annexation of abstract art, mini-skirts and rock'n'roll, as it has in Poland and Hungary, or will have generated deep, basic changes in the notion of Communist power.

America, America ... (1)

"And what about psychoanalysts?" a lady asked.

"I don't use them," I answered. "I don't need them."

"You don't?" she wondered. "What do you do when you want to talk, or when you need an explanation or advice? When you wish to communicate with a well-wishing soul? What do Europeans do in such situations?"

"We have our families or friends."

"How strange . . . ," whispered the lady sympathetically. She obviously considered us obsolete.

"And we still believe that abashment might be a factor of human quality," I added.

"Oh!" she sighed, evidently concerned with the poor shape of European psychological technology.

At once a proposition occurred to me: what if it turns out that modern American psychoanalysis is just psychology's Middle Ages, filled with witch hunts and grossly-conceived morality? What if it is simply the reign of endemic sorcerers of the soul? The Age of Enlightenment must come, and sense will win! Could we then avoid a bloody *réglement des comptes*? Could we prevent the situation in which remnants of America's trees will be decorated with psychoanalysts, hung by people who resent their dark powers and arrogant exploitation!

TOWER

In Biblical times, a tower—a vertical construction testifying to man's ability to elevate himself above the earth's level—symbolized a challenge to God's laws and a blasphemic attempt to overcome the natural condition. In Christian Middle Ages, a tower—a hauntingly artistic, gothic spire—expressed man's spiritual yearning, his sublime *élan* toward an Absolute and Divine located beyond our horizontal abode. In the Age of Enlightenment, and later in the era of Positivism, a tower—a powerful, iron structure erected by means of sound engineering techniques, experience, skill, and craftsmanship—manifested man's ability to subdue the law of gravitation and stubbornly triumph over dozens of minor physical laws, and thus announced a victorious human mastery over dozens of nature's secrets. Today a tower, according to psychoanalysts and their followers, is a phallic symbol.

From the center of a new, superb university campus, departing from its harmonious surroundings, stands a slim, proportionate, perfectly-perpendicular tower—a magnificent example of modern construction, building technology, and sophisticated materials. I liked it when first I saw it. Then I passed by with a young professor. "A phallic symbol," he said. "These architects want to reassure themselves of their masculinity, and so they impose their agonies on us." I strolled with a middle-aged woman teacher. "We women," she said quite aggressively, "are supposed to be constantly aware of men's superiority on this campus."—and she nodded at the tower lest I lean toward a different connotation of her words and be left to any meaningless ideas. "Why do you men always want to impress us!" sighed an attractive young girl leaving the faculty club with me. "Why aren't we left with some empty space in our consciousness to fill with mental associations other than that one?"

The lack of response from my side was met in all three cases with slightly concealed disapproval. I was helpless, being rather an unimaginative person with no need of a substitute, a compensation, or an excuse. For me, it was just a tower.

THE PILL

No one doubts that mankind has arrived at the stage where procreation and preservation of life are on the verge of turning against mankind itself. And God sent us the pill. Christianity has always believed in signs from Heaven. Saint Paul and Joan of Arc, among many, are the best witnesses. This wonderful ingredient of faith goes even further back—into the old Hebrew tradition. When the chosen people were plagued and endangered by adversities, God sent down either theoretical advice or practical help. Since Christ, all mankind is included in the "chosen people," but divine intervention has become very rare. Why not then accept with humble and joyful gratitude the recent intervention? Why does the Church hierarchy have difficulty understanding a phenomenon so obvious to the rank-and-file Catholic's comprehension?

THE POWER OF IMPERFECTION

It took me quite a while before I grasped a curious misconception of basic ideas, so predominant in some circles of American intelligentsia. I am far from unrestrainedly glorifying this country as I am fully aware of its traps. There are some moral and social features of America and the so-called *American* character and heritage, ideology, and set of values that evoke, rather, fright and repulsion, and that are conspicuous sources of mischief, misdeeds, and shame. It requires no exceptional perceptiveness to spot and reject them. They compel conscious individuals and groups to relentlessly fight for their eventual and final eradication. But it is also a common misdemeanor among domestic critics that they refuse to acknowledge that these faults are curable, or even to acknowledge that efforts have already been undertaken to cure them.

What is troublesome, for it is unjust and misconceived, is their penchant to accuse America or, more precisely, American democracy for all the ills and wrongs that, by nature, are connected to the very essence of life; ancient philosophers called it destiny or fate, coincidence or circumstance. The complexity of modern social infrastructures involves more newly-formed, dangerous issues unexpectedly related to ancient signs and denominators of man's *esse*. America Haters—and there are a number among Americans themselves, pretending to be merely opponents of the existing order—tend spitefully to blame American social imperfections only; they seem deaf, immune to any rational argument demonstrating irrelevancies between a man's misfortune in his struggle against social abuses and the American Constitution. They claim that they alone are able to delve into the depths of American insidiousness—a childish presumption. Practically, any new arrival rapidly realizes the limits of American manners and human respect, and how quickly they can turn into ignominious disregard for sensitivity and conscience in every branch of the moral and social panorama. But one should never lose one's fiduciary sense and label changeable elements of current processes immanent evil. Life, as *Ding an Sich*, surely contains immanent evils but until evil is institutionalized the imperfect can improve. One should not confuse that which is created by life with that created by men. One of the essential differences between democracy and totalitarianism is that, while many evils of the former derive from life itself, those of the latter are chiefly conceived and produced by men. One has to experience life within the framework of the Communist social order to perceive the meaning of institutionalized evil, created not from within—by life—but elaborated by man, imposed upon men, and used against them.

Generally, our epoch appears more ruthless and corrupt than any previous ones, giving more opportunities for evil, erecting more obstacles in the pursuit of decency. In some way it must have to do with the invention of the telephone or with the bottomless simplification of life's paradigm as interpreted in the modern press. Since the dawn of mankind, we have tried to defeat life's immanent evils: hate, disease, injustice, ignorance, violence, the fragility of human existence—both in the biological and the ontological sense. But we haven't scored many successes. Our golden era of technological wonders, mass media, and deliverance through permissiveness has added other heavy burdens to this list—psychological frustration, social alienation. Perhaps we shall never reach even that low degree of perfection where the wise and decent are hailed more loudly than the smart and slick, where goodness is deservedly celebrated and slyness branded. But those who have lived under any totalitarian system are firmly convinced that such progress is more possible within the disabled, crippled, flawed, faulty, at each step insulted, humiliated, subverted, undermined, slandered, vilified, besmirched, and despised American democracy than within any other system anywhere and at any time in history.

Some Remarks on History and Naiveté

I was walking down Madison Avenue. Somewhere in the fifties, in the womb of the world's most powerful propaganda machine, I became aware of its tender clumsiness. The titans of public relations' magic, the giants of the black art of advertising and publicity, devilish persuaders who with no effort can explain to the most obsessive cornflake hater that his future and happiness depends on its daily use and can force him to eat it every morning seemed quite as helpless as infants. For they are unable to deal with, annihilate, and avenge an extraordinary perfidy of which America, for decades, has been the victim.

No one who is sufficiently impartial and open-minded has any doubt that Russia's history, its growth in significance and dominance, have been based on continuous war and conquests, violent annexations, robbery and plunder, the capture and amassing of immense wealth at the expense of its neighbors; while the evolution of its political power, from the primitive to the most complex and sophisticated forms, has been founded on tyranny and slavery. No one who is sufficiently well-informed and unprejudiced would deny that American history, in addition to infamous deeds, involves economic growth, accumulations of wealth through industry and labor, territorial expansion through purchase, painful and often cruel implementation of human and social rights, and the trend toward abolishing forms of exploitation. In the twentieth century, the basic juxtaposition of the Russian gendarme versus the American merchant hasn't changed, except that the gendarme decided to enlighten the rest of the world that the merchant's output of goods, their effective distribution, and his consistent improvement in social mechanisms are equal to exploitation and oppression; but that political and military subjugation, misery, and ignominious submission of its own and of other nations are in fact a happy life in freedom and plenty. For fifty years, the pious adherents of the latest Russian state religion have promulgated this blatant nonsense everywhere, American universities and literary salons included. And America to this day, with its countless wizards of argumentation who are perfectly capable of convincing entire nations that a certain brand of toothpaste *is* their salvation, cannot defend itself against this calumny.

ATAVISM

The American male's erotic ideals in spite of the growing sexual revolution are still based on an ancient, traditional, American trapper's code of honor. The glory, pride, and relish is to kill as many as possible of the hunted creatures, no matter whether they can be delighted in and consumed properly in more refined ways. History has taught us that even such a species as the American buffalo was unable to endure this kind of treatment and so gave up and became extinct.

AMERICA, AMERICA ... (2)

In Europe, a beggar's declaration of need is: 'Please, support a poor man who just wants to buy a slice of bread, sir."

An American beggar asks: "Could you spare a dime for a cup of coffee, sir? Or a quarter for a beer? Since yesterday, I haven't had a drop in my mouth."

In Europe, a beggar who would dare suggest a handout for other than nutritive reasons would be crushed by his society's indignation. In America, food has already failed as the stuff of charity. A handout has been promoted from a weapon against starvation to an instrument against a lack in one's well-being.

New York—or the Disregard for Sadness

For centuries, sadness has held a prominent position in European cities. Paris, Rome, Vienna, or Warsaw have room for all kinds of melancholy moods. They are provided with small, perennial *cafés*, sentimental benches not far from a river, old weathered bridges, picturesque cemeteries, and gloomy park corners and alleys—chiseled by age, literature, and tradition—where poets could timelessly sit and offer themselves to sadness. Sad feelings, romantic poses, fashionable distress, literary spleen, bottomless *chandra*, decorative *cafard*, distinguished *Weltschmerz*, pathetic attitude—these can be practiced and cultivated only in such spots. New York is devoid of them. All we can find here are places in which we can perfect despair.

Ideology

The reception was chic, and people communicated with no obligations. For a few minutes I faced a tall, well-dressed man with a superb mustache; he was related to me only through the metaphysics of a cocktail party. He looked quite waspish and was endowed with that special dash of boredom and cheerfulness which characterizes some members of the American upper class. He mumbled a small something; I had difficulty getting his remarks.

"Where are you from?" he asked rather indifferently. I told him where I was from.

"What are you doing in this country?" he wished to know. I told him what I'm doing here.

"When are you going back?" he continued without any apparent deeper interest, only to keep up the conversation.

"It's hard to say," I answered. "Some twenty, thirty years from now. I've applied for permanent residence."

"Well," he said "welcome aboard."

This open acceptance was unexpected, and I must have looked startled, because he added: "You know, after all, each of us came to this country once. Three generations earlier, or later, what does it matter? Let's drift along together."

3.

Israeli Notebook

ATHENS–LYDDA

In Athens people had complained of the most unbearable heat in years. We landed in Lydda around 10:00 P.M. The sticky, strangling air bowed me close to the ground when I left the plane. Athens' scorching airport flickered in my mind like an oasis of zephyrous freshness. "How can people live here?" was my first reaction. I learned later that they can and even with an unexpected grandeur.

TEL-AVIV

The stubborn, burning desire to be—to survive, to exist—has always been the substance of Jewish history. It has turned into political fact in this most hazy political epoch when nations and states are and are not at the same time. Few would deny, I hope, that we face the existence of some states and nations that practically do not exist at all. But Israel is and exists and is present everywhere: in display windows of its maritime line on the Avenue de l'Opera in Paris, at every airport in Western

Europe with its modern air service, on every radio program with *Hava Nagila*. The Magen David banner waves throughout the world at youth festivals, musical events, cardiologists' international gatherings, chess championships, and commercial expositions. It is familiar, hated, despised by its perennial foes and despisers, but it is present. We may worry about what is precarious and insecure in this existence: we may be troubled that its very being is questioned. But it *is*, it *exists*. Unlike, for example, Bulgaria, which exists, but is not. . . .

🌿 *Israel* is probably the last bulwark of the small-grocery-shop civilization. Ideology, politics, economy, and public life depend here on the "have a little chat" formula. Every deed is, in the end, accommodated to the "a Jew is a Jew wherever he may be" principle, which, when applied to the functional, administrative hierarchy, humanizes and, at the same time, weakens, the state's structure. Everything is mitigated by the sacred liturgy of selling pumpkin seeds and the admiration granted the honest, dignified retail business. The small grocery shop was an institution in the Eastern European *shtetl*; it cultivated some moral and social virtues, like an excessive, not necessarily sincere, but ever-obliging cordiality; like social solidarity and readiness to help. Even the *kibbutzim* —perhaps the mightiest factor in shaping the contemporary Israeli consciousness—whose moral, philosophical, and mental habits should have challenged the small-grocery-shop mentality, did not escape its powerful influence. Everything in Israel is still linked to atavistic, cultural roots, everything with the exception of the army. The army was with the Jews neither in the Eastern European *shtetl* nor on the Stock Exchanges of Paris, London, and Frankfurt. The army despises, hates, and mercilessly fights the spirit of the small grocery shop in the souls of the Israelis. One may say that the result of this fight will be the future of the state.

❧ *The heat* is unbearable, and when I arrive for dinner at an airy, comfortable Tel-Aviv apartment, my host says:
"You may take your jacket off."
"I would prefer to keep it on," I answer.
The host: "But it's terribly hot tonight."
Me: "Oh, yes, it's awfully hot. I know."
The host, rather insistingly: "Take it off. You *don't know* how hot it is. . . ."

❧ *A common quarrel* in a public place, a routine clash at the post office, differences of opinion in a crowded bus make evident the tragicomedy of a huge social group forced to acquire a new tongue. As is widely known, politenesses are always the easiest phrases to conquer in an alien language. Hebrew words *b'vakasha* (please) and *toda* (thanks) are easy to learn, and every new Israeli knows them immediately. It's amusing to listen to two quarreling newcomers; their capacity to insult each other is limited to awkward uses of polite words.

❧ *In their papers*, books, and countless discussions, the Israelis are mainly concerned with the amalgam of spiritual, mental, and moral qualities (characteristics, virtues, and even drawbacks) that distinguish them from the Jews. In my opinion, this trend is already becoming a cliché. It is time now to emphasize what they have in common with Jews. It is obvious that Israel is and must be a focused product of the transmutation of Jews into Israelis—too much is at stake to forget it—but the Jews, Jewishness, and all that has been accumulated during the more than two thousand years of Diaspora should not undergo ruthless elimination on the grounds of deserved resentment. The ability to turn every defeat into victory is a crucial skill in organizing a nation's consciousness; the British were and are masters of that astuteness. It sounds cynical, but it does bring a period of blessed psychological relaxation to every community struggling for its peremptory *raison d'état* of common survival.

JAFFA

I went to Jaffa, a magnificent example of one of the oldest cities in mankind's history but is unable to exploit its own value. I arrived at a square, marked Hagana Square on my city plan. But as I came to the street sign, it revealed another name. I approached a policeman standing in the middle of the square; he was young, strongly-built, sunburned, and looked surprisingly neat in the gluey damp heat of the afternoon. I asked: "Could you tell me—is this Hagana Square?"

He smiled vaguely, with a kind of melancholic overtone; I thought I had the wrong impression as my simple question would not make a normal cop on duty nostalgic. Then he answered: "It should be."

I must admit that this reply roused mixed feelings in me. I had never heard such imprecise information. Nevertheless, the problem became somewhat complex, obviously involving some unexpected elements, both of reason and emotion, not to be solved by simple cartographic explanation alone. I hesitated a moment to form a certain attitude towards the new situation created by the incertitude of my informer. Then I said rather helplessly: "But something must be done with this square? With its name at least. Is it Hagana Square, or isn't it?"

"It is, and it isn't," answered the policeman firmly, and the firmness in his voice forced me once more in life to think about the unlimited violence of relativity. His answer was definite and founded on some unshakable truth, and as far as everyone should know the many faces of the simplest truth, the policeman smiled at me in a kind of deserved triumph. I grinned, nodded, and went away.

Then it occurred to me to what awesome depths the two answers of the policeman pierced. The square was once called Hagana Square, but later the name was changed. Hagana, as is known, is the symbol of a most respected memory of the recent past; heroism and sacrifice and the noble romanticism of Israel's successful struggle for freedom are incorporated into this word. It may have been the policeman was a Hagana man himself? Perhaps his most glorious days passed in closest attachment to that sound? And surely he *is* a worshiping nationalist who could hardly agree with City Hall's decision to change the square's name. But at the same time he could not deny the existing reality. Trying not to be unfaithful to his own conviction and yet not to misinform me, he chose to avoid a clash with directness, which, as we are all aware, is most deceptive. He entered the vast margin of allusion, the only possibility of being honest, the first duty of a policeman.

TEL-AVIV

The bitterness of the disappointed—one feels it at every step. They are more numerous than I expected, more strikingly present than in any other country. It is understandable. One must only look at the mighty intellectual potential of this country. Every other waiter or bus driver thinks he is fit for something better than he's doing. And they resent life for harming them by not giving them what they deserve. The one blames fortune, the other people, most, language. Language is the cause of failures, breakdowns, even tragedies.

❦ *The accouterments* of military equipment are worn here as accessories *à la mode*. Israel must be the last country where the idea of the frontier, patterned after the American tradition, is living and prospering. Pioneerism is an idealistic and patriotic attitude and, at the same time, a vogue. This is a country where a popular fashion implies moral virtues. There are few societies in the world that can boast that its youth consider courage, sacrifice, and duty *chic*.

❧ *There is much talk* about what a fascinating melting pot of diverse quasi-national elements, habits, and manners makes up the new, emerging society of Israel. I would caution against excessive hopes being founded on the melting-pot theory; Israel already represents a functional society, though not yet a structural one. The constructive process is still going on, the structure is in the process of becoming, in the creation stage. The existence of many separate substructures can be easily observed, and their social substance acts against the melting-pot conception. Instead of a mingling and forging of alien elements, one feels the hidden, camouflaged but bitter struggle for domination. It may sound ruthless, but the sooner one of these substructures succeeds in subjugating all the others, the sounder the building of the society will be, and the quicker it may proceed. For the healthy collective consciousness of a nation can never be based on sentimental premises.

In terms of sheer numbers of social groups, this small nation exceeds many others. The old pioneers and the young *sabras*, the Yemenite Jews and the Sefardim, the Ashkenazim and the Orthodox, the Chaluzzim, the kibbutzniks and the state administration, the Levantine Jews and the trade unions—all these groups are distinct and often antagonistic. They form a magnetic bundle of social classes, civilizations, ideologies, and problems that could give a powerful headache to the social leaders of a much larger country. Let's, for example, tackle the problem of the prosperous Ashkenazi Jews who consider themselves the main economic force—and with good reason. They do not constitute any ideological authority; they grew up with the refusal of ideology in Central and Eastern Europe, where religion (approached more as tradition than faith) and an anti-Semitic environment were the forging ties. Theodor Herzl had trouble galvanizing their Jewishness; Adolf Hitler did it better. Throughout the centuries, they developed a high civilization and intellectual standard, established a great culture and many social values of which they can be proud. In Israel, their nationalistic indifference vanished only to a certain limit, but their children fought in the Liberation War and formed needed leadership in many branches of Israel's life. They are not well liked today, but their homes and the coffee-shops where they gather serve as focal points and patterns for imitation. Snobbery was always a precious element of social advance and never should be underestimated. Probably this is the end of the road for the thousand years of European Ashkenazi Jewry.

❧ *If you ask* an Israeli waiter: "May I have a glass of water?" he answers: "Why not?"

An immediate stimulus to a ceaseless exchange of ideas!

❧ *No other nation* can match the Jewish record for long-standing persecution. This causes a peculiar psychological atmosphere in today's Israel. People become inebriated on mere lack of persecution. The state is exposed to many dangers, but persecution is not a danger here. Yet one thinks that nations normally get drunk with joy at victories, not that they would be satisfied with only the elimination of a disaster.

❧ *Everyone asks*: "How do you like *our* country?"
What's strange is: this mouthed, turgid, insisting, and
artificial question sounds sincere and moving.

❧ *Each public place*—bus station, post office, and so
forth—is an amusing denial of the race theory in a most
spectacular way: a Spanish grandee, a Russian peasant, a
Mediterranean Levantine, and a Prussian Junker stand in
the same line, and they all are Jews.

❧ *"Adonij,"* said one Israeli to me, "a stupidity that is
successful ends by being accepted as the big wisdom. . . ."
We spoke of Russian social achievements, the French
anti-novel, and the Arab political dialectic.

BEERSHEBA

On the road one can observe figures representing
the most fantastic cocktail of civilizations: an old Jew
with corkscrew curls and long gray beard, in skullcap and
Lee's blue jeans, sits on a modern bulldozer and builds the
highway to Beersheba. . . .

SHEFER-ZOHAR—DEAD SEA

What today seem simple, obvious, even banal objects of love and hate were taught mankind in the Bible.
At the dawn of human conscience and awareness they
were revelations. In the meantime a good many moral
categories have been worn away on the paths of history
or damaged by the ruinous relativism of philosophy. We
of this century face the necessity either of renewing them
or inventing values to replace them. Here not far from
Sodom, I am obsessed by a hazy uncrystallized reflection
that on this soil this old/new nation (catalyzed by weird,
unique historical processes, arrived back on the same
rough, severe piece of land) has more possibilities and

opportunities to bring humanity a New Word than the mightiest centers of contemporary political, economic, and cultural power. Its moral, religious, and social problems may smell of *provincia*, but they are capable of evolving into a ferment of the Grand, Unexpected, and Important.

Ein Gedi

Many of the Bible's features were artistically aggrandized: the proverbial holocaust of three hundred thousand Amalekites by the Hebrews could be reduced to some three hundred dead and wounded. Probably all those wars and struggles were major brawls; the kings and generals disposed of a strength-potentiality of gang chiefs; even in the perspective of their world, the scale of possibility was extremely limited and provincial. The pettiness of the stakes they fought for was miserable: a herd of rams, a pasturage, a piece of land equal to a district.

And what a literature evolved! What an intellectual and artistic masterpiece!

Eilat—Red Sea

There is a nightclub in Eilat picturesquely called "The End of the World Club." I tried to find it, and I couldn't. I was unable, in spite of all efforts, to reach the end of the world during the day. All around were plenty of *shikuns*—cooperative housing settlements—and courtyards full of playing children.

❧ *Eilat* is the most incredible conglomeration of pioneerism and decadent sophistication. Rough Israeli frontier soldiers sit on the beach next to the most abnegated and extravagant Scandinavian hippies. Against such a background, the hippies are reminiscent of the depraved and refined, Virginia-born gamblers in Arizona saloons in the 1870s.

TIMNA

I went to Timna, King Solomon's copper mines, on a guided tour. Our guide was very fluent; he looked like a homosexual playboy from a *chic* Florida beach. What amazed me was the tone of deep sincerity in his patriotic statements: all that he spoke was saturated with an ardent patriotism that could easily be taken for professional propaganda. But it was not. When we parted I asked him why a man of his eloquence (in Hebrew, English, and French!) stays in such a God-forlorn, primitive spot like Eilat. His "I love it here" sounded artificial but convincing.

TEL-AVIV

The attitude towards Germans: the older generation who lived through the war in Europe still desires the blood of every living German. Good or bad Germans do not exist—every one they saw then in Europe wanted to murder them, and now they want revenge. The impossibility of forgiveness is obvious to them, but incommunicable to others, as everything their eyes saw is impossible to describe to others. The younger generation knows perfectly well how the Germans were and how to judge the past, but they meet German youths who come to Israel in search of redemption and expiation of their fathers' sins, who agree humbly with every expression of hate and repulsion, who work hard in the kibbutzim and eat at separate tables as they are not accepted. It is much easier to doom nations than to hate individuals, who may be repugnant as representatives of guilt but who are not guilty themselves. The Israeli youth must somehow deal with this enormous and complex problem.

❧ *Israel is a crossroads* of grandeur and shoddiness. The ancient is magnificent and moving, the new—moving and littered. There are superb edifices and tasteful luxury hotels, along with entire areas of rubbish and trumpery. One may say: "That's usual in the Orient," but the Israeli does not consider his an Oriental country and with good reason. Besides, it's a country ruled by social democrats, a welfare state where social contrasts theoretically should not occur. The impression of general disrepair may be due to the climate but, paradoxically enough, the monuments of the past look splendid, neat, well-preserved, and they inspire respect. I wandered once with an Englishman through London's Queen Street, cleaned and polished like a surgeon's room, and there was one cigarette butt on the sidewalk. "Impossible," murmured the Briton, "to stroll in this filthy city. . . ." I wandered some months later with an Israeli friend through Allenby in Tel-Aviv, which does not resemble a surgeon's room at all. "Couldn't it be cleaned up a little here?" I asked. "Such a principal avenue . . ." "You are an anti-Semite," he retorted.

❧ *The basic denial* of the personification of God, the bulwark of Hebrew tradition, religion and *Weltanschauung*, resulted obviously in a deep-rooted contempt for the material in Jewish ideological heritage. As always in life, the Jews were constantly accused of being the bearers of materialism considered as the worship of money, despite the fact that the most effective champion of philosophical materialism, Karl Marx (a Jew), was evangelically poor. The Jews' perennial *l'amour de l'argent* was rather a symbolism, a substitute for the worldly power of which they were deprived. The claim of Jewish materialism was based on Jewish successes in the world of commerce, business and finance, but the Jewish ability to succeed came more from the sense of abstract thinking and speculative reasoning. Their merchant talent derived chiefly from the mystical predisposition to talmudic (or scholastic?) meditation; their passion for bargaining is really a passion for discussion and analysis.

If materialism equals the concrete—the world of things, the sense of structural practicalism, the need of social hierarchy, and the love of organized matter, Jews never developed such qualities, never had any historical occasion to shape them. They do now in Israel. But it is not easy to erase two thousand years from a people's mentality, to erase efficiently what was praised, cherished, and adored throughout centuries. The Jewish necessity for quest may be a promise of the greatest accomplishments. "If you find an inscription in Europe 'Private Road,' you're sure no one will enter," someone said. "But you may be also sure that the first passing Jew will. Here we have a country whose whole population compulsively enters where it is prohibited." Apart from the fact that he was not right—the degree of social discipline seemed to me higher than elsewhere, probably as the result of the never ceasing war menace—I feel optimistic about this characteristic; it may cause trouble to the administration but offers an opportunity to human expectations. Perhaps once more this poor, not very ordered, tiny slice of land will breed The New.

❧ *The sheruth taxi* is an Israeli specialty—a collective taxi service. It is usually a large, old fashioned car that takes six or eight persons going in the same direction. The fare is a little more than a bus. When I entered a *sheruth*, five people were already there. I addressed the driver in English. One of the passengers asked: "Where are you from?"

"Poland," I answered.

"From Communist Poland?" wondered an old woman.

"Today's Poland is governed by the Marxists, indeed," I said diplomatically.

"When did you come to the country?" a man in front of me wanted to know.

"Some weeks ago."

"Are you going back?" my collocutor was interested.

"You know . . . ," I murmured, "things like that are rather a matter of private consideration . . ."

"Why should he not go back?" a man with an olive complexion turned to face us.

"And why should he go?" the woman said, excited. "What does a man like that have to do in Communism?"

"Don't tell him he'll be better here," sneered the olive-faced.

"And what is wrong with this country?" aggressively asked a young girl, silent until now. "I don't like talk like that! Are you a Jew or what?" she addressed the olive face.

"I can not see such an enormous *glick* in being a Jew," said the driver. "Especially when the whole day I have to listen to such idiotic blab as now."

"You're not going to insult me for my money," said the woman. "Stop the car, I'm getting off."

The driver stopped and turned to the woman. I slipped him a pound and left hastily. I looked a while from a safe distance at them. The woman did not leave. The driver started and went off. When they passed by, I could still hear loud voices. I never entered a *sheruth* again.

JERUSALEM

Light, flaxen stones and dusty-green olive trees. There are contents and values in the air, basic and elemental, the rudiments of our whole being. A cradle of that which is so violently evident in our mind and soul that to try to express it would be in vain.

JERUSALEM—YAD VASHEM

The memorial to millions of Jews murdered by the Germans. An architectural, simple shape, structured in a rock. One cannot stop one's tears upon entering. One can't help thinking that if anti-Semitism, one of mankind's ugliest diseases, is abating, it is redeemed with the warm blood of all those dead, not long ago.

4.

From the Spanish Notebook

CIUDAD REAL

The very heart of the Spanish continent. There is the same powerfully good smell on the streets of this provincial Castilian town as in Madrid and Toledo. It is the men who smell so good—the males. A strong smell of not-always-refined perfume follows them when they pass. It would be interesting to know what they distrust so. Their own hygiene? Is it the general abhorrence of the body? Their mistrust may originate from the ancient traditional awareness of the filth of the flesh, a medieval conviction that man's body is the abode of the worst fetor, an attitude toward the human form easy to see in the paintings of Ribera and Zurbarán. In Spain, Christianity was always connected with a deep contempt for the body, unable to free itself from ugliness, deformity, faults, and abomination. In fact, the Middle Ages here were one huge stench, diffused in the churches by incense. The church, although still very mighty, has lost some of its power of persuasion and soothing. The cosmetic industry has taken its place.

CORDOBA

My modest Pensión de San Luis is located in one of the narrowest streets in Cordoba, and has a classic, shabby but clean, eighteenth-century patio. The thick, serene, July night air wraps the patio in navy blue cotton. The innkeeper (from Cervantes) and local parson (from Gustave Doré) sit watching a TV broadcast of the San Fermin festivities. Hemingway wrote his brilliant description of Pamplona during San Fermin just in time. Thirty years later he might have had difficulties selling it to a publisher. Yet Hemingway's version is a thousand times more accurate and interesting than TV's artistic illiteracy. Again I'm struck by the misery of contemporary ways of shaping man's imagination, this precious source of our successes on this earth.

SEVILLE

It is a natural birthplace for the theater. Every wall fragment, little street and square, bend, and corner is a stage setting for a dramatic plot. Each scene inspires dramatic fancy. Here, there, and everywhere in these streets, Figaro might shave and Carmen dance.

Only here could the myth of Don Juan be born, conceived out of the perennial lack of erotic satisfaction among the males. For a Spaniard it is a miraculous legend about a man who had too many women, who was free to choose among them, then toss them away. In this country where a woman guards her chastity with fierce stubbornness and shrewdness—for if she loses it by accident or through passion, her life ends in a sewer—woman's revenge upon men is formidable. Men spend hours sitting in the coffee houses, sentimentally holding hands (exaltation of friendship, not deviation!), sublimating their sensualism at the *corridas*. But they can screw only their wives or whores. Hence the dreams about Don Juan and his adventures. Not until Central Europe invented psychoanalysis was it declared that Don Juan was perhaps simply impotent.

GRANADA

I saw my first corrida in Madrid. After the first few minutes of initial excitement, caused by the sight and smell of blood and general gore in the atmosphere, I began feeling bored. An incessant series of killings and deaths is finally as monotonous as any repeated motif of life and art. My ears inflamed, I felt that mean, abject satisfaction of witnessing a cruel, dirty finish to natural existence, which pins one's attention to the most repulsive spectacle, even when the observer is sick to his stomach. Overcome by a sense of the grotesque, I also felt distant from it, safe from spiritual engagement or genuine, sensual participation. Bulls jumped into the ring, filled with reckless, kinetic energy, and later were carried away by horses. In between, there was a transition from the jumping, dynamic, mindless, pulsating being to the blood-covered plethora of animal matter. And what of the famous, glorified part of man in the undertaking? I had read countless descriptions of the ritualistic, graceful ballet performance of the toreadors, their mystic tradition, their liturgy of killing, their courage and almost religious sense of challenge. And above all, I've read and heard praise of their passion in risking their lives and safety at every minute in the fight. But here my opposition was born. I don't wish to sound contemptuous, nor to deny the historical list of victims, but I think every activity or profession that involves killing has to deal with the same perils. A butcher is trained to kill without inflicting harm to himself, but a nervous, unskilled butcher can easily chop his arm off. Anyone who has the slightest knowledge of boxing—primarily the art of avoiding and blocking blows—immediately recognizes the relative ease of the *torero's* task: a bull reminds one of a boxer who operates exclusively with an uppercut; a skilled *torero* (who has firmly decided not to be mutilated) is able to avoid his hits endlessly. And here was the abuse, the gimmick, or the fraud. I wouldn't like watching a fistfight in which only one of the boxers was able to use his uppercut while the other could swing punches from every possible angle, even if he exposed himself in an extravagant, audacious, and slightly clownish way.

I've gone to *corridas* since, in Seville and Granada, for I felt I had not found the most important and decisive reason for my rejection. I was especially puzzled that thousands of people, women and children (I among them) get accustomed to violent death and agony, joking and laughing when the fumes of blood and slaughter are distinctly visible in the big animal's last breath. Lovers hold hands, children lick ice cream, mothers feed infants, married people quarrel, and I glance around for goodlooking girls. Would it be possible when witnessing a horse's death? Could we behave the same way watching the agony of a dog or a chicken? We humans who are consciously aware of the exceptionality of death? Probably plenty of these people were not capable of assisting at the drowning of kittens, not to mention at the hunting of elephants by natives in Africa.

Then it occurred to me. It was really very simple. The bull is the only animal, and surely the only mammal, that dies without protest against death. It dies like an heroic human being ashamed of the ugliness of anguish and agony. Many times I saw an awkward *torero*, unable to kill with that famous hit of mercy which cuts life off instantly; his sword hacks the bull's throat, veins, aorta, and the animal is immobilized—it stands awhile, as if knowing the inevitable destiny; while blood streams in torrents through its nostrils, it does not try to escape its doom. Then slowly, beautifully, it collapses on already powerless forelegs. And most pathetic and moving—the bull dies *silently*. Every animal with enough power to scream, cry, thrash about, shuffle, rampage, does it; only the bull ends with no sound. He fought, he lost, he accepts his fate with dignity. The contrast between the violent vitality of the mass of muscles a few minutes before and its sudden, quiet resignation is appeasing. It erases our feelings of guilt, of harm done. If the bull tried to crawl away, to moan, to jerk, to howl like every turkey and every wolf, we would be overcome by pity and horror. But the bull cares for attitude, pride, immaculate honor, and heroism, which makes its death *spectacular* and thus *bearable*, but evokes no compassion. We humans eagerly witness the end of grandeur but rarely are very emotional about it.

The bull's silence in death was discovered ages ago by the Spaniards; they have used it to create a national pastime.

Madrid

Being a bootblack is nowhere a very honorable occupation; but in Spain, any situation where one human being must polish the shoes of another is deeply humiliating. I would be unfair if I insisted that the humiliation is chiefly a product of the one whose shoe is being polished: he does sit in the most insolent and insulting pose, lolling at the coffeehouse table, conversing, and indicating clearly by his behavior what little meaning that human rag at his feet has for the rest of the universe. But something must be said in his defense: look at the obvious shamelessness of the one who polishes! He behaves in a strange way—he doesn't show the discreet abashment of a European shoeshine boy, nor the democratic *hutzpah* and *cameraderie* of a little Negro from the

New York streets, nor the menial cringing of an Oriental. He apparently finds masochistic pleasure in his humiliation; it gives him the legitimate right to hate the loller. And justified hatred is, perhaps, a most refined delight of the Spanish soul.

5.

A European from America in Europe

DEPARTURE AND ARRIVAL

Quite an uneasy feeling—I feel European but I am no more. Cathedrals and Giordano Bruno, Lorelei, Flaubert, Chopin, Buckingham Palace, and Gorgonzola still have meaning for me, a blend of tender snobbery with uppish sentimentalism. And I am fully aware of the hidden contents in Tuscan chapels and Copenhagen's urban landscape that are missing from American chapels and angular maps of American cities. But European university halls and auditoriums lack something that American campuses are filled with—a special kind of involvement in mankind's tormented present, crucial for the shaping of the future.

THE REALM OF THINGS

There is something in the structural pattern in the American realm of things that makes an object—tree, railway, car, bridge, water tower, horizon—look differently from a similar one in Europe. Certainly objects vary according to regions, and a window, chair, or kettle

changes its form and character with each European country. Nevertheless, they are all European. After forty years
of conscious European existence, I prefer the American
version of an elevator, a mule cart, and the sense of
privacy.

DOCTRINE

Doctrine is the essence, nucleus, and core of
European civilization. Americans dared build a civilization upon the simple premise that it is better to make
things better than to arrange them according to a doctrine. Until the end of their days as inhabitants of an
independent continent, Europeans will never pardon
them.

THE GIANT SHADOW CAST ACROSS THE OCEAN

Every European has an overwhelming awareness
of America's existence, not only as a powerful political
factor whose decisions can influence the historical issues,
but as an omnipresent entity whose heterogeneous radia-
tion affects every sphere of experience, in mental as well
as material ways. In Europe, everyone lives *with* America.
An imaginary belief that everything is better in America
is somehow ingrained in the European consciousness.
This is all but impossible to explain to anyone who was
not a European by birth. One should not too hastily forget
that the Argonauts were Europeans.

SITTING IN A PARIS COFFEEHOUSE

Sitting in a Paris coffeehouse, which is an ideological attitude, reading a Paris journal, watching a Paris
street, it appears that America is a stronghold of seriousness. For a whole epoch, a paper nose and clownish straw
hat symbolized America in the eyes of many Europeans.
I agree that there is plenty of naïveté in the American
Weltanschauung; America's vision of life and the world,

chiefly as mirrored in its press, often bears the mark of insupportable simplism. But American pragmatic idealism is serious, its moral endeavor solid. By comparison, the European pretense to omniscience seems childish.

On Paris Students Revolution

It's difficult and thankless to try acting as *sans-culottes* in an age of *prêt à porter* (ready-to-wear).

Introduction to Geo-Sandwichology

The complexities of the current geopolitical situation can be easily deduced from the difference between sandwiches. I daresay that the concept of a sandwich symbolizes the basic gap between our two continents. In Europe, they eat bread with some ham, cheese, liverwurst, or whatever. In America, we eat ham, cheese, liverwurst, or whatever with just an insignificant bit, a traditional touch of bread.

New Social Awareness and the Shampoo

"*I do not want freedom,*" a visitor from Eastern Europe told me in Paris. "I'm afraid of it. I feel old and tired. Freedom means choice, the possibility of estimating and the necessity to select. It also means constant effort in judging and evaluating life's ways, attitudes, and stands. It opens the perennial question: 'Who am I and where go I?' which can be answered in so many ways that it gives me a headache. In Communist Eastern Europe, I'm perfectly aware of who I am and what I can or cannot do, which is the perimeter of my functions and desires. My telephone is bugged, but I know it; it's a blessed certitude, and I'm not exposed to improper temptations of intimacy. Freedom here is a nauseous multitude of shampoos among which I have to choose. I don't want so many!

I want one under government control, very difficult to find and obtain. My needs and wishes then make sense. This we call peace of mind."

I was impressed by his torment. I did not mention, of course, that the plenitude of shampoos in America makes the French stock look as if it were under government control.

THE SAINT-GERMAIN-EN-LAYE FOREST

I am not affected by monuments any longer, but nature remains a source of infinite sentimentalism. Trees, moss, dead leaves, bark, revoke echoes of delicate familiarity. The color of the sky, the smell and transparency of the air—which created European painting—are, for a moment, so dear to me.

AN ELEGY

A Frenchman told me the following story:

"Late in the night I entered an empty *bistro* in the *Faubourg Poissonnière* neighborhood. I slowly drank my coffee next to an old man who was short and worn out. Across the street, two adolescents in leather jackets were covering a wall with graffiti: *US = SS . . . Vietcong shall win!!!* The old man sighed and said: 'Why do they do such things? That's not good, that's wrong and mean. I am an old Jew, a furrier. My father, God bless his soul, came here from Odessa, escaping the Russian *pogroms*. He wanted to go to America but we did not have enough money. America, my father used to repeat, is a refuge for the persecuted, hunted, oppressed, poor, sick, and weak. It's a promised land, a shield of God against evil. When evil rises, America sends us help. Soldiers or money come here and rescue us. We look to America with hope as to a land of plenty and justice for all those who need it. Why do those boys slander America? Don't they realize that they are trampling on our feelings? We won't ever believe that the US and SS are the same! Never, never, never . . . ,' he repeated over and over again, almost hysterically."

"And what did you tell him?" I asked my French friend.

"I'm an existentialist," he smiled, "and I did not feel like mediating between an old, sentimental simpleton and two young Communist barbarians."

Optimism

August Comte once wrote: "Humanity—it is more the dead than the living."

When I found and reread this sentence, an influx of inappropriate good humor overcame me. I'm sure I'm not the first who has culled some comfort from this notion.

Artists

Meeting European ladies and gentlemen who practice any creative profession, I notice their concern for acclaim in America. This is not only a matter of substantial income delight. Simply, success in Europe is no longer enough. During the twenties and thirties, a *name* acquired in Europe still generated awestruck sighs in American literary salons. Today an American artist doesn't mind being acknowledged in Europe. He finds it pleasant. But truly and intensely, he needs and seeks acclaim in America.

Feydeau at Marigny

Feydeau is a little French Shakespeare *au ridicule*. He created his own universe filled with precise notions of guilt and virtue. It doesn't matter that his world is constructed upon the arch-principle of universal idiocy; it is still a complete world. It mirrors life, even if its texture is pure, hypernatural ludicrousness. Feydeau's theater *boulevardier* epitomizes French passion for what describes the phrase: *"c'est une bonne histoire."* The French are superb and incomparable when acting Feydeau. It's fascinating how much a nation, so sober, rationalistic, calculating, so permeated with the worship of dry logic, is able to do for the sake of *une bonne histoire* . . .

RIDDLES OF GEOGRAPHY

I'm sitting before the desk of a French publisher, playing absentmindedly with a little, plastic Scotch tape set. The trademark reads: "Made in France by Minnesota de France."

What does it mean? Do we have two Minnesotas? Do we export them? Do the French have one?

This tiny inscription seems to me more to the point than the famous book of Mr. Servan-Schreiber entitled *Le défi Américain.*

PRESENTIMENT

I have misgivings that a quarter of a century of calm and peacefulness is all Europe can hold out for. Today Europe is wary, skeptical, meticulous but, at the same time, abrasive and chafed like an aging, frustrated woman who, after a life full of pleasure and fulfillment, suddenly realizes that everything is over and never to come again. When talking to Western Europeans under twenty-five years of age, I'm frightened by their senseless preparedness to accept any grim, insipid lie disguised as a remedy, their readiness to destroy liberties for which they have not fought, their contempt for an affluence for which they have not worked or sweated. I begin to doubt whether the Marshall Plan was, in fact, a thoroughly successful move. Looking at young German leftists who, having escaped the East German, oppressive totalitarianism, violently demonstrate against the social system that endows them with the right to express their opinions, I ask myself: where do aberrations end? Aging, embittered beauties are dangerously prone to create any complication to satisfy their uncontrolled passion, to embrace every flicker of hope that it might be as it was in the past. Kissed by youthful idiots, who care only about getting them easily to bed, they imagine themselves to possess ageless wisdom of unbeatable magnitude. And we are already twenty-three years after the end of the World War II. . . .

MYSTERIES OF MEDICINE

"*England*," someone told me in France, "is the old sick man of contemporary Europe."

"France," someone told me in England, "is the old sick man of contemporary Europe."

I didn't express my opinion in either case. So far as I remember, both countries are of feminine gender in their respective languages.

WISDOM THAT INSPIRES AWE

I saw rather few mini-skirts on Parisian streets. When asked, a young, attractive girl answered thoughtfully: "I think the knee an extremely important part of the female body. One has to be much careful in handling it."

FRANCE

A hundred years ago or more, France was loved in Europe. "I love France more than my own country!" was as common an exclamation in aristocratic salons as in literary coffeehouses across the continent. For those who dabbled in arts and letters, aspired to elegance, sighed for frivolous hedonism, or cherished popular and revolu-

tionary traditions, France constituted an adopted mother-
land.

Today it would be venturesome to maintain that France
is still loved. But in some remarkable way, this country
has preserved, in spite of all its failure and meanness, an
unquestionable charm. At closer scrutiny, one discovers
that it's the weight of France's history and literature. Anyone sensitive to history and literature is immediately con-
quered. In these tenements, narrow and deliciously dirty,
they all lived—from François Villon through Manon Les-
caut and Emma Bovary to Rimbaud and Swann. We cannot help thinking of that.

In New York, we try to accumulate a similar charm in
some parts of the city, but we fall victim to an expanding
economy that does not allow the harboring of a tenant
for such a long time.

POCKETBOOK STRUCTURALISM

The seventeenth-century Frenchman was widely
known for his courtesy and his distinguished taste; he
considered amiability a supreme virtue. At the same time,
he was the most feared warrior in his contemporary
world. The nineteenth-century Frenchman lived in a cult
of bravado but still preserved chevalieresque gestures and
a devotion to noble politeness. And still he was highly
regarded on the battlefields. The modern Frenchman
adores what he calls toughness, a pretended readiness to
bousculade or *bagarre*. At each step, he sees himself as
un dur de durs even if in reality he's only a somnolent
bookkeeper. If you stop at a gas station, the attendant
springs out like a fighting-spirited Jimmy Cagney, holding his hose like a gun. In the most serene *bistros*, everyone talks in that specific tone of the bad guys at a saloon
counter in early John Ford movies.

During the twentieth-century, the French have lost all

their wars, except those in which they were helped by others.

Auto-(mobile)-cracy

In America, cars are inoffensive. Save their annoying number, they do not constitute a threat to man's supremacy over objects. Europe is under the cars' occupation. Automobiles are noisy and aggressive, despite their lamentable size. They behave as if they were out of human control. They are overtly against men. They rule in a most oppressive way.

Paris

It is a great city. A superb, grandiose, splendid city. Probably the most beautiful city in the world. But it's also a city where periodicals called *Historia Magazine*, *Historama*, *Mirroir de l'Histoire* are sold at newspaper stands on every street corner.

Saint Sulpice

Of all Paris churches, the church of Saint Sulpice is most touchingly meaningful for me. When in Paris, I always spend a few minutes sitting in its dark, somber, powerful nave. I leave it with my nostalgia restored—it is a nostalgia for that kind of Frenchness that dematerializes so quickly in our time. The heavy greatness of this church symbolizes somehow for me the congruence of might with suffering. It is the last witness of the peculiar epoch of the Musketeers, when brutal force still mixed well with coquetry.

Morals and Manners

A driver is, for an American, another human being. A pedestrian is too. For an unmounted European, a driver is a murderer; for a European behind the wheel, a passerby is his personal, bloodthirsty enemy whom he is summoned to kill, injure, or at least deprive of dignity. The holy war between drivers and marchers still ravages European backward civilization. Until this paleozoic stage has passed, any progress toward modern culture is out of reach.

THE END OF THREE DECADES

For thirty years from time to time, irregularly but doggedly, I have passed the corner of *Boulevard Saint-Michel* and *rue de Pantheon* and stopped for a while to muse. For decades, I preserved the serene faith that nothing changes here, except a few neon lights. I was wrong, for the world changes. Traditionally, I entered a little shop called *Chanteclair*, stepped down a spiral staircase, picked up a pair of vintage earphones and listened blissfully to a Chick Webb record featuring Ella Fitzgerald in "A tisket, a tasket . . ."

This year I didn't get the perennial support of the ageless charms of the Swing Era. Downstairs was an ugly boutique, with pop art and aggrandized Campbell Soup cans as the embodiments of a new charm.

THE MOVIES

On Champs-Élysées people are standing in line for two movie houses. Ont of them is presenting a film described on the posters as the story of a male virgin. I can imagine why people look forward to seeing it. The second line, more numerous, is in front of a cinema presenting "Bonnie and Clyde." What do Frenchmen expect to find? American cruelty? Fun? Their own moral superiority? Or their dreams?

OFFICES

It is the sad fate of some old palaces in Europe to be converted into offices. Superbly emblazoned ceilings, walls covered with subtle reliefs, priceless wood panelings must live together with metal cabinet files, formica-topped desks and Woolworth-sold coat hooks. But when Americans build airy, poetically-inspired palaces for offices, they are often accused of being tasteless.

AMERICAN IDEALISM

Europeans sn. ?r at me when I speak about American idealism. This sneering is a source of bewilderment to me. Future historians will probably call our century a time of giving, America being the giver and Europe, since 1917, the unhappy, embittered recipient. In some remote corners of Europe, people still wear trouser belts from American World War I military outfits, open their cans with can openers from World War II Care parcels, and sleep on YMCA mattresses—melancholy remnants of the tremendous number of goods America poured into Europe during the last fifty years. Certainly, one should not confuse political deeds with idealism, but how should one label giving without any hope of return or even gratitude?

The sneering comes mainly from the half-educated, helpless news consumers and pub politicians. The more sophisticated smile ironically. Materialism and individualism, they argue, have marked the American way of life from its beginning, and these two notions contradict idealism, especially in its social aspect. This blab about materialism and individualism seems to me obsolete, shallow nineteenth-century stuff, a lot of poor clichés having little in common with the present state of affairs. The American socioeconomic syndrome, although evolving from a worship of production and an egoistic sense of *laissez-faire*, at certain times undoubtedly ruthless, immoral and chaotic, was transmuted finally into a principle: Help another to establish himself for you may profit by it. Support your neighbor because his prosperity is your prosperity—the old, colonial rule—underlay the widely displayed idolatry of relentless free competition for an entire century. At this point, Europeans may chuckle sarcastically and ask: "But what has all this to do with idealism? The motivation is profit and prosperity, not ideals." Here begins European narrowness and inability to see beyond ossified doctrinairism. The continent that invented pessimism, tragedy, a theory of devouring species, *Wille zur Macht* and existentialism, and cradled Schopenhauer and Kirkegaard, refuses to recognize natural links existing between idealism and optimism, especially if the former bears some practical overtones and the latter prefers to be cautious, even calculating. European societies for centuries have lived under the heavy burden of such antisocial feelings as envy, jealousy, malevolence. Initiative, a spirit of innovation, and inventiveness are regarded by many as personal offenses easily formulated in a hypocritically concealed credo: Why should I help another and let him get ahead of me, make more money, or become more famous? No one claims these feelings do not exist in America; they form a part of eternal human nature and are as legitimately present in America as everywhere else. However, they never determined the social pattern of behavior in America but are secondary to the usual troubles of humanness and the human condition. In many European countries, on the other hand, among many of its peoples, the practice of "clipping" or "pinioning wings" became the very fabric of a social reality that emerges with unexpected force in countless intimate conversations with disillusioned and embittered Europeans. American unwillingness to cut off initiative may sometimes take extreme proportions: after one of the race riots, a New York policeman, responding to accusations of the law enforcers' apathetic attitude in the face of arson and looting, allegedly said: "No one will catch me shooting at those poor kids just because they grab TV sets worth some lousy couple of hundred thousand dollars. . . ." If this is not sufficient antimaterialistic idealism I don't know what is. I wonder how the police of such idealistic countries (with a sense of personal ownership) like France and Italy would react facing looters in Galeries Lafayette or in Via del Corso. Not to mention the carnage that would occur if some members of an idealistic Communist nation (with a newly developed sense of sacrosanct state property) should try to acquire some state-owned goods directly from the windows of Moscow's Univermag or Warsaw's Central Department Store.

It's true, as America-haters say, that it is possible to sell everything in America. One should only add that it is true of generosity too, and also the highest moral values. It only means that this kind of output easily finds customers and purchasers. One can make an excellent living if one has a good, sympathetic heart to offer, or compassion, or charitable character, or altruism and helpfulness. Why should idealism overlook the advantages of a perfectly functioning, booming economy? It forms a new social and moral power, difficult to grasp by petrified, European notions. Perhaps someone will try to detect irony in these words but I honestly consider it an apotheosis.

SUNGLASSES

Sunglasses are a most cultivated mark of elegance in warm, sunny countries, proving once more that fashion is still a form of self-defense.

BRITISH WOMEN

After British men lost the Empire and decided to withdraw from the world scene, British women jumped into the ring of history. Led by daring and inventive power seekers in many fields, they started a struggle for the survival of Britishness in today's civilization. But having been absent for centuries from the foreground of British culture, they were burdened with the flaws of every newcomer. They made the mistakes and slipped into the vulgarity typical of the *nouveau riche* and the social climbers.

L'Entente Cordiale

L'Entente Cordiale, that determined the last sixty years of British–French relations, has diminished to a relationship better denoted as *Nonchalance Empoisonnée*. There is a tone of venomous, ill-wishing mockery in what the French say about the Britons, and vice versa. It evokes the epoch that succeeded the Middle Ages' bitter hatreds, the times of Richelieu and Samuel Pepys, when they spoke reciprocally about *le roi d'Angleterre* and the French court with superbly accentuated mistrust and gallant disdain but still admired their respective achievements in philosophy, cabinetwork, cheese preparation, shipbuilding, and fashion. The difference between then and now lies mostly in an essential lack of achievements, except that concerning fashion and cheese.

An Embarrassing Situation

Britain today reminds one of a person who was well off his whole life, but in his old days has come to know he is much poorer than he ever imagined one could be.

Strange Sadness of Neo-Dandyism

Long-legged, mini-skirted, stylishly-underfed girls sit, stroll, or browse in boutiques on Piccadilly Circus or Carnaby Street, looking dully at space filled with a blown-up Lord Kitchener's face and other British camp, humming along with eunuchoid, amplified Beatles' voices. The boutiques contain the objects of a new faith cult that I would call neo-dandyism. Embroidered males in grotesque shirts, serving customers, seem in search of implementing their sacrosanct vision of life. As with every embryonic and meager set of philosophical axioms, neo-dandyism treasures little but a priceless awareness of its uniqueness and a spirit of innovation. This is its saddest error. Beards, locks, and nudity are nothing new, and they never aided any revolution of human culture. Their forefathers erected a tremendous empire by selling kettles and knives to the savages—a bold and inventive occupation expressing great sociotechnological changes in mankind's history. The grandsons try to sell psychedelic mugs to the tourists from Midlands.

THE BIG SALE

We are currently witnessing the sale of an enormous empire. It was the second empire in history constructed on purely national qualities. The first was the Romans'. All other empires were won either by one man's genius and will, or by a consuming belief that one religion was better than another. The British, like the Romans, were conquering pragmatists utterly convinced of their own superiority. The fact that they succeeded in building the vastest of all known empires proves that they were somewhat right. It looks like the time of empires built with the support of ethnic values is over. Future empires will be ideological or scientific. Of course, they will not breed Stevensons, Kiplings, or Conrads any more, but when the time comes, who will care?

THE COURT OF SAINT JAMES' BOND

The endless flow of spy literature and movies from England must have deeper than purely commercial reasons. Probably it is a psychological substitute for the lost position in world politics that the British try to replace with imaginary influence. Five hundred years of involvement in global political intricacies has left a feeling of nostalgia. Being a shaping factor no more, they try to recreate its sweet delights in fiction. The new Soviet empire fills the empty place left by the loss of Colonel Lawrence's hunting grounds in Asia; the KGB and MVD are a new version of Bengal Stranglers; and the complexity and opaqueness of Communist social and human relations is their recompense for the lost African jungle. Dismissing themselves from responsibility in world affairs, they can afford a total lack of authenticity; it helps with the thriller technique and gives the possibility of erasing old British failures by creating new myths. After centuries of the worst cuisine in Europe, and after fame for splendid indifference in sex matters, the Englishman emerges from an espionage novel of the sixties as a fine gourmet and irresistible seducer. One of the authors has his hero proudly confess his coquettish diseases of gluttony and satyriasis. Yet during the effervescently developing plot, his wild erotomania is easily calmed by two intercourses throughout two hundred and thirty pages.

JAZZ

The British have an amazing sense of Dixieland music. This phenomenon is difficult to explain, notwithstanding some superficial clues. An old beggar in an ageless London cap, bringing to mind the first meeting of Professor Higgins with Eliza Doolittle, stands in front of the Tottenham Court Road tube station with a battered banjo in hand—and swings like mad.

A HAYMARKET ECOUNTER

I stood at the corner of Picadilly Circus and Haymarket, relishing the quintessential street perspectives when my attention was pinned to something that gave me a momentary feeling of jubilant familiarity. It was a man walking cheerfully down Haymarket, with that inimitable pace of a country gentleman visiting London. He was all tweed, mustache, ruddy complexion, crumpled wool hat, tartan, porcelain eyes, cavalry twill, and a cherry tree stick. He was an archetype, an embodiment, and a symbol, stepping out from the pages of P. G. Wodehouse's collected works—a most poignant glorification of his species. For my generation of Eastern Europeans, he personified a mark of excellence, one destined by four centuries of literature, horse-breeding, and Home Fleet to be envied and worshipped by the rest of mankind, and indefeasible in Western civilization's portfolio of values. Indefeasible? For the first time in my life, my watchful, admiring look, my instantaneous impulse of appreciation, was somehow uncertain. For the first time, I detected something I wouldn't have dared suspect. It was shabbiness. For the first time in my life, a specimen I always secretly wished to identify with looked to me shabby-genteel.

And it came to my mind how everything English looks superb on Park Avenue and 57th Street. The Burberrys and Wedgwood, Rolls Royces, bowler hats, and Church's shoes. I presume that even these days, such a British country gentleman would look better in America.

More on the Mini-skirt

The boundaries of the empire shrink and, by some mystic coincidence, the hemline goes up. Men went into forced retirement and an astounding number of good-looking girls appeared on the streets of London. Britain always lacked good-looking girls, the pass-by-and-look-back kind, the charming flora of European cities. The Continentals always accused the Englishwoman of masculinity, generating thousands of dubious jokes. Currently, the Englishwoman is taking her revenge, but clumsily, in my opinion. By inventing mini-skirts and the most modern style of coyness, she doesn't gain the status of sophisticated femininity. Rather, she achieves a new notion of girlishness. It's hard to claim that a mini-skirt is not sexy; certainly it is, but it isn't feminine. And the stripping of an Englishwoman's femininity continues; with every month, the hemline is lifted higher, pushing an English girl into the category of a child. In her rapid career, she seems to have forgotten that a female child is more amusing than interesting. As a matter of fact, there is something cheerless and dismal in a mini-skirt as seen in Britain, the country of its origin. There is an effort to attract that diminishes attraction, an attempt to be gay that compromises gaiety, a striving for liberty that involves permissiveness, an endeavor to recover lost fun that stresses intensity where it should never be manifest.

CARNABY STREET

A new empire of style? A proud attempt to replace the perfidy of Albion with mod alarm clocks, *divide et impera* with checkered bellbottom trousers, "wait and see" with black leather motorcycle jackets, and *Britannia rules the waves* with sets of incense?

A FRAGMENT OF CONVERSATION WITH A CONCERNED EUROPEAN

He: "*If we want to give* to our youth a paradigm, or simile, or pattern of how to live, we have to delve into this century's American literature—Hemingway, for example. European outlines from the same period have been proven ridiculous: either the poetic nonsense of existentialism without any practical bearing on our daily existence, or the open idiocy of socialist realism. We do do not have our own valid prescription for the moment."

I: "But Hemingway was rather a romanticist, not a very deep one, who indicated more how to behave in certain situations than how to live. And you have, for example, a Saint-Exupéry whose personality and writings are priceless collections of indications how to live."

He: "Yes, but do you know the difference between an American refrigerator and a European one? The former works better and is easier to handle. It's true of paradigms —they are only successful when they are constructed for common use, fit for shrewd publicity, and easy to accept."

I: "Why, then, is Europe unable to produce its own?"

He: "We have lost all sense of guilt. That is what originates any morality, social or individual. You at least have your Vietnam and your race problem. Their weight, importance and complexity makes them all global issues. And they give you a feeling of real, precious guilt. And what do we have? The Common Market and *La Chamade*?"

BLUE JEANS

Blue jeans equal the dress of the epoch. They are also the most visible mark of evidence of how fundamentally Europe has been influenced, in both culture and civilization, by America. Blue jeans constitute a style of life, and we know how easily ideologies derive from style. A Polish adolescent, once asked why he paid the total of his monthly maintenance for a pair of genuine Levis, difficult to obtain in Communist Poland, said: "One can imagine living without hope, love, or happiness, but it's thoroughly impossible to exist without blue jeans any more. You're not accepted as a human being." Blue jeans pass unnoticed in America, as a natural part of the landscape. But their impact, distinction, and particular significance in Europe are strikingly noticeable.

AMERICA'S CHARISMA

All over Europe, we run across some Marx Brothers *à la française*, Italian versions of pop art, Finnish answers to William Faulkner, Czech renditions of "St. Louis Blues," Greek counterparts of Paul Newman, or West German impersonations of Wyatt Earp. In this country, we imitate neither Jean-Paul Sartre nor Fernandel. We read one and watch the other on the screen, substantially increasing their material well being. It's perhaps the reason for Sartre's eagerness to vilify America at each step with such petty, provincial ignorance.

AN EPISODE

Aboard a suburban train from Maisons-Laffitte to the Gare Saint-Lazare in Paris. According to French social stratification, suburbia equals modesty more than luxury, as the cream of the upper-middle class lives midtown. The train was gently imbued with a garlic smell emanating in equal proportions from workers as well as *petit-bourgeois*. A drunken clod of a man who, on the station platform, was already on everyone's nerves, was delivering an obscene soliloquy in which he strived to express some political beliefs and his personal disgust with women. I belong, as a rule, to those fortunates who, in such situations, are immediately the depositories of an alcoholic's, or mentally disturbed person's, confessions; hence, it was quite natural that the man took his place next to me to pour out his grievances and to spread around me his foul breath. Fatalistically, I am also a compulsive answerer to these who struggle with life's meaninglessness; thus, I pronounced a few words in my not-too-brushed-up French, consequently turning his penetrating mind away from the relativity of existence and focusing it on the more tangible problem of foreigners in *la belle France*.

With new force, he delved into a monologue about the abjectness of each not-French-born creature, accusing each of moral and physical filth, and explaining to me, and to the rest of the car, what a plague foreigners, *les métèques*, are and how perversely they poison and destroy the flawless set of natural French values. And at the top of any foreign depravity, he pointed out Americans who, as shameless tourists, sponge on his country's marvels and, as hideous invaders, murder children in Vietnam. Then with a thundering voice, attracting the attention of the entire car, he asked: "And who are you? What's your nationality?"

I answered: "American."

Now, as a matter of fact, I'm only a permanent resident of the United States and, neither legally nor morally, do I have any right to call myself an American. It would have been ludicrous, however, to go into the complexities of immigration regulations; the moment demanded action. Under special circumstances morality and legality become secondary, and we act according to the legitimacy of emotions. And in this French suburban train, in the midst of the garlic smell and the mocking hostility, my feelings were unequivocal. "You crucify people in Vietnam!" shouted the man, and I began to prepare myself for an uneven fight and humiliation when the train stopped at Gare St. Lazare, and people rushed out.

I moved along the platform as a short, tidy person in a *béret basque*, whom I had noticed earlier in the car, caught up with me and said: "*Excusez-moi, Monsieur*, I just wanted to tell you how sorry I felt. But as you surely know, there are morons in every country all over the world. . . ."

6.

On Revolution—

and Related Matters

THE INDOMITABLE FLAWLESSNESS OF DAWN

Scientists are not certain when man invented the wheel—a circular frame or disk designed to revolve on an axis—that revolutionized his notions of distance and weight. They presume it occurred sometime during the Neolithic period of the Holocene era, six thousand to ten thousand years ago. But they generally agree that it was the most difficult invention in civilization's history with an importance overshadowing anything man had ever done before or after. It took an infinitely longer time to achieve, if counted from the species' very beginning, than it took afterwards to construct a combustion engine or split the atom. Yet this device, both conceived and applied by hirsute Stone Age thinkers, still serves superbly. One has only to imagine the most refined Cadillac or the most powerful armored division propelling over a hard surface without wheels. For all its technological miracles, mankind has been unable to replace the wheel with anything better or improved. I have always been impressed by its weird, hoary, never-extinct usefulness that leads to the question: perhaps it hasn't been necessary to replace it? Perhaps the wheel's form, essence, and nature are ultimate, and only its functions can be continually increased and perfected. The idea that an early happening might remain timelessly applicable doesn't appear much *en vogue* of late, but that's that.

The principle of the core of democracy is not very much younger than that of the wheel. A power of decision drawn from the majority, with the ever-open possibility of a minority turning into a majority, seems not totally alien to the earliest communities of *homo sapiens*. Century after century, new features were added to the rudimentary pattern, as countless men of thought and of action commented on and enriched its sense and substance. Unlimited abuses and outrages were committed in its name, or against it, but the fundamental principle remained sound and unchanging. The most potent human brains argued successfully that the power of the majority equals immorality, stupidity, and callousness, that it smells foul and strips the human being of both dignity and progress. But whatever *they* advocated and suggested revealed itself to be worse. Others attempted to endow democracy with a new sort of excellence; the final effects were much like improving the wheel by shaping it into an octagon. "The true freedom exists only in the place where there is no ordinary freedom . . ."—once wrote an Eastern European playwright with bitter irony. The same goes for democracy. I'm afraid that no possibility exists of inventing anything better than the ordinary democracy, for simply nothing better exists. What is left is the endless possibility of increasing and perfecting its functions, in the same way that made the wheel an organic element of our reality.

CHILDREN OF THE CENTURY AND
HEROES OF OUR TIME

The adolescent American revolutionary of today
is a repetition. He has a predecessor—the Romantic rebel
of the first quarter of the nineteenth century. Their ideals
and thought processes are similar. Their behavioral pattern is all but identical. The texture of their lives tends to
have plenty in common. Even their concepts of outward
accessories and symbols bear striking resemblances to
one another.

The Romantic rebel turned against the insensitiveness
embodied, in his eyes, in his contemporaries, against society and its postfeudal system, against political tyranny
and the blights he perceived in oncoming industrializa-
tion. He culled pride from his lofty loneliness, then the
fashionable word for alienation. His was a contempt for
conventions and order, and for all other bonds except the
natural ones. He yearned for individual distinction, proving oneself, flights of ambition, fresh impulses of the
heart, intensity of emotion and action. He had his passionate chroniclers, some of them the literary geniuses
of his epoch. Goethe, Byron, Pushkin, Alfred de Vigny
perpetuated his memorable traits. By sheer force of their
art, they monumentalized both his virtues and his ridiculous aspects. They widened the gap between him and his
environment more than it really existed—a great publicity
hat trick, so skilfully pulled off by the American press of
late—because nothing attracts better than the much-
advertised partisanship of the attractive, or mythology
disguised as reporting. Alfred de Musset coined for him
a proud and tender formula: *l'Enfant du Siècle*, Mikhail
Lermontov called him more forcefully: *Geroj Nashego
Vremeni* or a "Hero of our Time." They made of him the
style of an era, a notion encompassing everything from
Weltanschauung to hairdo, a paradigm to be followed by

those who craved for glossily prescribed and codified ideals for instant use.

He was also persecuted by those he had been combating, but not too severely. The feudal and monarchic structures were antique and in transition. They felt old and tired and were indulgent and skeptical about the set of values they were supposed to protect. They reveled in solid political machinations, malicious wisdom, and irony. A rebel had to have perpetrated a serious misdeed or offense to be seriously stricken. The monarchs and the governments bestowed upon revolutionaries all kinds of compromises and courtesies, passports, exit visas when needed, and mild punishments that made heroes out of them for a song. They flirted with them, praised their audacity, invited them to courts, encouraged their effronteries, bantered with them, and perversely helped to build up their public image.

History proved that the Romantic rebellion was more reactionary than progressive. Its hard-core followers consistently turned against civilization and finally despaired of any progress. In a more distant future, their decadent antirationalism was to feed many of the ideological premises of Fascism and Nazism. Meanwhile, the crumbling monarchic orders went constitutional, became cradles of modern liberalism, positivism, and scientific advancement, developed industries and humanitarianism, and coddled the best traditions of tolerant restraint and social forbearance.

There were also other heroes at the time, but they were less conspicuous, more modest, and often accused of opportunism. Some of them were busy with extracting great secrets of life from nature, others contributed significantly to various branches of science, conquering disease, and extending human life. Thereby they contributed, indirectly but certainly, to the fact that, when the next, very recent edition of the heroes-of-our-time appeared on the world scene, they were already mass-produced and infinitely more numerous.

The distinctive difference between the Romantic and the hero of our time lies in the sense of pride. The former wanted to fight and to bear all consequences of the struggle. He considered feudalism an evil, scorned it, wanted nothing from it, and recognized its right to fight back in self-defense. Being chiefly of aristocratic origin, the Romantic rebel cared about dignity and knew that only in his readiness to pay the full price would it be given to him. He welcomed persecution, for it adorned his fight with moral legitimacy. On the other hand, the hero of our time demands all possible privileges from the order he tries to shatter. He claims the right to ruin without any responsibility, and as a matter of fact he even asks for the *right* to annihilate from those he desires to annihilate. Their resistance he calls oppression. Their arguments in defense of themselves and their values, he brands as opportunism and presents as the sinful corruption and the uttermost degradation of the American social system. Hence, what do you call it when someone who is beaten up for some abuse that he proclaims a virtue vilifies his tamer, forgetfully omitting to mention that he attacked first in order to bite off the other's ear. A Romanic rebel would have called it a lack of dignity, and perhaps would also have added the adjective "squalid."

THE VICISSITUDE OF ORDER

Whatever youth perceives makes sense. Conversely to maturity's awareness of a messy *déjà vu* that subverts every meaning. Youth has a mystic sense of order. It's the most important reason for the young's compulsion to revolt against order at each step. For someone young, the world has an ordered meaning, things and ideas fit into well-classified compartments, strict evaluations contain an inward logic and are worthy of belief. The slightest abuse, borne by imaginative inexperience, legitimates revolt.

People of age have an overwhelming, though not always conscious, sense of life's anarchy. This is the main reason why they hopelessly yearn for order and constantly accuse youth of creating disorder and anarchy.

The Inevitable And The Unacceptable

No revolution ever resulted in moral transformation; that is, no revolution ever changed human nature or any of life's inherent evils into anything better. Revolutions change banners, colors, inscriptions, and ways of life, called by purists social conditions. Even if part of a population appreciates the new, postrevolutionary condition, it soon comes to find out that only the form, not the content, of their lives has been affected. Success is the only social factor that revolutions seriously tackle: as a rule, one who is successful before a revolution is rarely supposed to be afterwards. As a matter of course, this rule is usually violated in the most intricate ways, and the history of social change is interspersed with prerevolutionary reactionaries who made prestigious careers after a turnover. Career is largely the effect of personal abilities geared into favorable circumstances—which plain, simpleminded people call good luck or smartness—and revolutionary idealism has proved too faint a force to deal with successfully.

Some think of revolutions as epileptic diseases, inflicting the most horrible sufferings on the convulsed body. History, however, indicates that the due process of convalescence and recuperation from their appalling consequences gives way to all those feebly determined values others call progress. Healing their wounds turns into what can be defined as achievement. Nonetheless, it's almost inconceivable to imagine today's world without its previous revolutions. For centuries, our sages blandly but doggedly have insisted that we are doomed to be wrong. Never are we permitted to choose between good and bad, but only between better and worse. This is what all revolutionaries (reformers as well) should keep in mind. The sociopolitical possibilities of the human race are as limited by gravity as one's body is. This doesn't absolve us from the imperative and privilege of seeking change, but not without being aware of the most simple truth that change in itself can by no means be a supreme value. Nothing, though, frees us from pursuing what we consider right, or fighting against that which we see as wrong. It does become boring after a time, but not before thirty-five.

Brief Encounter

On the bus heading toward the university campus, I met a girl with a folded-up red flag. She was blackhaired and myopic. "Hi, Dolores," said my companion to her. And he whispered to me: "Spanish names are chic among revolutionaries nowadays. Not Russian any more . . ."

"What a nice color," I said, pointing to the fabric.

"It's the color of fighting socialism," the girl said.

"Is that so?" I felt well instructed.

"I'm a Socialist," she added proudly.

I said: "Congratulations . . . ," which sounded rather silly, but I wanted somehow to honor her adamant devotion to the cause. A bit vexed, she shrugged and said: "Well, what could *you* possibly know about socialism?"

"Not much," I admitted. "I only lived twenty years in a socialist country."

"And what of that?" she said with open scorn. "What did you see there, what did you learn from it? For me, twenty days in Moscow was enough to recognize how beautiful it is! Beautiful, beautiful, beautiful . . . ," she repeated, as a sort of voluptuous beatitude covered her face. "How interesting," I thought, "it would be to locate that delicate membrane that separates bliss from idiocy."

ART, POLITICS, AND SOCIAL CONSCIENCE

Having acquired position, but also a New-York-style-awareness of the sociophilosophical ills of our time, a young artist from Texas declared during a press interview: "All people are political prisoners in the sense that they are prisoners of the system into which they are born."

It's hard to deny that the above sentence is an impressive example of thinking. It would be interesting, though, to know what the thinker thinks about specific countries and systems where men spend half of their lives in prisons because they think that a human individual has the unquestionable right to think freely. And what our pundit thinks about the strange circumstances that in his own country, with its political system, he does not risk being imprisoned for whatever he thinks, even if he shapes his ideas in a blatantly preposterous way from both a logical and semantic point of view, and then expresses them in word and print.

PROFESSOR MARCUSE

Reading Professor Marcuse, one gets a notion of him as a distinguished intellectual who has been spared the bare necessity of surviving Hitler and Stalin, a dismal eventuality that has not been spared many intellectuals in Europe, and who therefore now feels frustrated. He is called the father of the modern youth revolution. This parentage might prove the cause of revolution's miserable performance. Anger, despair, determination, and fanaticism have generated revolutions until now but never frustration, which might be held solely responsible for fashionable attitudes, poses, and countenances. According to Mr. Marcuse, air pollution is one of the most destructive elements of repressive American capitalism, as it is organized by the inhuman incorporated monsters whom revolution is authorized to annihilate mercilessly. Air pollution considered as an instrument of social oppression is of dubious value, when it is noticed that the oppressors are forced to inhale it as we do. The arguments used by Mr. Marcuse in his neodialectical manual of upheaval and transmogrification do not qualify him as a redoubtable opponent, but rather as a symbol of the modern mind's colorful restlessness—very handy for public manifestations and press releases—somewhat like the Beatles in the earlier era of rock music.

TYRMAND'S LAW

I wish to see my name, henceforth and forever, connected to a law that I discovered and formulated— namely:

The quality of a revolutionary is inversely proportional to the system he fights against—the more oppressive and cruel the system, the more heroic and self-sacrificing is the rebel; in other words, the better and more indulgent the system, the more flippant the revolutionary.

Of course, as with every natural law, I didn't invent or shape it, but merely uncovered an aspect of reality that my contemporaries stubbornly refuse to see. Each social system and each system of values has always had its revolutionaries. But in societies with a long-time democratic tradition of free expression, their qualitative assessment gets hopelessly muddled by the shallowness of perfunctory press reports and interpretation. Resisting a policeman who is trying to drag an occupant out of a university building can by no means be called heroism. The young Russian intelligentsia struggles heroically for a clearly-defined set of liberties, which the young American intelligentsia actually fully enjoys. Young Russians pay for their demands with long-term jail sentences, concentration-camp tortures, wrecked lives, ruined health. They have their heroes—Sinyavskis, Daniels, Litvinovs, Ginsburgs. It would be interesting to ask whom the Western student rebellion could cast as a counterpart. Maybe the London Maoist student armed with a stupendous gadget that covers his face with red paint the moment a policeman approaches or press photographers zero their cameras in on him. The American campus warriors love to draw an equation between themselves and Czech students, but the latter could hardly recognize them as comrades. The young Czech desperately fights for the basic right to protest, a right his American analogue fully possesses but considers a minor asset and consequently abuses. The word "freedom" has a different meaning for each of them; for a Czech it is a value for which he is willing to risk his life; for the American rebel, it's a most natural condition, like breathing, that passes unnoticed unless it's put into words. Marking himself an opponent of the regime during his studies, a young Russian or Czech is disgracefully expelled from his university, canceling any possible chance for a reasonable existence. Spending his period of education on revolutionary activities, an American student heads toward a bright future: his nonconformity is usually acknowledged as a sign of brilliance; he is hailed for stirring up parochial environments, destroying mental stalemates, and his rebel spirit is called a freshness of ideas that enriches the prospects of progress. As a rule and *a priori*, he is attributed a *positive* role in society, and if after studies he does not commit himself to bomb-throwing, he is assured of obtaining an excellent job and benefit from his bloodthirsty past, either as a newly converted moderate, or as an intransigent firebrand making a posh living catering revolution to other affluent revolutionaries. A paper published by rebellious students in New York, sports a proud caption under its title: "1968—The Year of the Heroic Guerilla." Heroic? What's heroic about a fight whose consequences can be annulled with fifty dollars bail?

I do not try to belittle anything. All I want to say is that it's not true when some hypocritical reconciliators say that *both* systems are equally bad and *both* establishments are equally criminal. It doesn't require a very sharp eye to perceive that *one* of them is much better in every respect. A social reality in which one who wants to rectify society by force can enjoy personal freedom for the financial equivalent of a blazer is infinitely more valuable than a system in which one has to pay with his life for the same intention.

HATE ME OR LEAVE ME ...

"*I hate America,*" a lady said while tasting a bite of duckling to assure herself that it was properly crisp and tender. "America is a combination of insidiousness and churlishness." She sipped a bit of wine with careful attention so as to be prepared for any nasty surprises that a bottle of Pauillac (good year) might conceal. "Life is no more possible here under the inhuman pressure of corporative mammoth structures." She was good-looking, well-groomed, in her middle-age, and several times married, each time to someone wealthier than his predecessor. "The incessant impact of devilishly organized repression suffocates your individuality here," she added with persuasive certitude. "Even being peaceful and impartial, one is gripped by an imperative to fight against this blight, to revolt, to change it. The only hope are those poor, oppressed kids at the universities who know so well what they want and how to want it."

I felt an influx of sympathy and compassion, much stimulated by her flawless complexion. "And what about leaving the United States?" I looked for a solution. "Perhaps life somewhere else would give you a sense of meaningful existence?"

"Never," she said firmly. "This is my country. I hate it, but I also hate to hate it, which is very optimistic and good of me. I find a lot of comfort in my positive, constructive hatred."

"Of course," I agreed. "It may even be turned into a successful state of mind, at least from the financial point of view. There are several writers and playwrights, chiefly of foreign origin and citizenship, who make an excellent living exhibiting their hatred and contempt of America in print and word. They call it bold and constructive criticism. The more they hate and scorn, the larger their readership and audiences on Broadway. I wonder how they reconcile their bottomless disdain with accumulating money. Yet, spitting on America has proven the best way to obtain a substantial income for a foreign artist in this country. The most undeserved insults sell best."

"That goes with our best traditions," she said thoughtfully. "America is ludicrously provincial, and people in the provinces are too hypocritical to admit their abjectness and faulty institutions. Hence, only people from the outside tell them the truth."

"But their readiness to pay for it seems to me quite worldly," I sighed. "Besides, how do the haters see the truth from the Himalayas of their uppish, pseudointellectual disgust, or when blinded by hatred?"

"And what should we do with all the money?" she said slightingly. "There is enough of it going to all those fake, anti-Communist front organizations. We are smothered by our inability to counteract them, once more confirming our oppressors' hideous smartness."

"You're admirable . . . ," I confessed. "I won't ever grasp how it happens that modest, overworked, poorly dressed, underdogged people adore this country, and those who receive all from it, hate it?"

"Very simple," she said. "We are sensitive. Radicalism—that is sensitivity."

"This would be too simple," I sighed deeper. "Radicalism is a very complex, psychologically inexplicable impotence to concede to someone else's reason, to agree with him even if there is objective truth in his argument. In my opinion you live in the United States, because American democracy constitutes *a better reality in every respect* than any other sociopolitical reality in today's world, be it Western European societies, Russian, Cuban, or Chinese Communism."

"Nonsense," she retorted.

"Oh, no," I smiled. "Being an America-hater you are by nature incapable of admitting that America can be better than anything. It's incompatible with your innermost beliefs and your preconceived set of norms. But for me, intellectual superstition is the worst of all prejudices. Capitalism appears to be one of the most discredited words in the modern vocabulary; nevertheless, it's to be said quite overtly that, after one century of experience, it has proved to be better than socialism. I know that such a statement can only provoke shrugs; yet capitalism comes out as more flexible and apt to change according to life's needs, claims, and demands than socialism, as we know it from its various, contemporary versions. Moreover, and this seems to me quite decisive, capitalism transforms faster in practice than Socialism does in theory, which may turn out to be lethal for the latter. You can hate capitalism and America, such an attitude may contain even a dash of provocative charm, but I'm afraid the facts of life are against you . . ."

In spite of all my efforts, fully detached from politics and dialectic, I never dined with this lady again.

A Statement

I do not think that American society is sound, well functioning, law-abiding, moral-minded, and with equal opportunities for everyone. But at least it is probably the only one that tries hard to be such a one, and certainly the only one that scores some points in this game.

Credo

I have decided myself to defend America against itself. According to a long-established tradition, the American intellectual elite is its severest critic, prosecutor, and scoffer. This actually is one of the mightiest sources of American social and cultural vitality, as, in a general way, dynamic intellectual ferment constitutes a priceless element for renewal and progress. America's defender remains the simpleminded man on the street, emotionally confused and rationally inept, lowbrow in his ambitions and predilections, unable to cope with complexities, helpless before the formidable dialectical challenge. Someone has to help him. What a tremendous task! The chores are immense, but so are the prospects of success.

The Nostalgia of Wilting Ideas

"*Isn't it frightening*," a concerned, law-abiding citizen said to me. "They are young, dynamic, rapacious. What can we do? We are helpless in the face of their voracious and victorious youth."

"I wouldn't say that," I said. "Youth is their handicap and their weakness. History doesn't register any successful, full-scale revolution of youth, by youth, and for youth. Revolutions have to be heterogeneous to succeed.

It's impossible to have them without aged farmers and middle-aged housewives, not to mention men of all ages. Youth is too feeble a token to mobilize the forces necessary for an upheaval. Besides, time passes. A generation's revolution is always hopelessly vulnerable because of its very transience. The revolutionaries will form a pathetic association of former worshippers of unfulfilled expectations before they know it."

PROGRESS AND REVOLUTION

Does revolution have an ingredient of progress and renewal?

I think so. Revolutions usually take place in lackluster, shabby, worn-out settings—unhappy countries, overcrowded cities, rotten public edifices, slum neighborhoods —the decay (or ugliness or narrowness or cramped conditions) of which constitutes a legitimate reason for revolution. During the ensuing upheaval, the settings turn into shambles—or, at least, are sufficiently damaged to undergo extensive repair and painting once the revolution either is successfully suppressed or regrettably runs out of steam. I would call renovation a fair benefit of a revolution. This may be endangered only by the *victory* of the revolution. Under that condition, the shabbiness is meticulously preserved, to serve as evidence of the pre-revolutionary misery and hence as moral justification for having overthrown the system. Sometimes everything remains exactly as it was in the past but is declared better than before, with everyone being forced to repeat that such-and-such a house or street is bright and spacious, even though it is as filthy and cramped as it ever was.

THE MALAISE OF THE VOID

They are poor and helpless, the young, and hence desperate. They have to rely on trivial shams that we have already had time to investigate and classify as trivial shams, if not as criminal blunders, and they will have to pay for their blind devotion to slogans and half-truths sooner or later, as many have paid before them. They are filled with lofty emptiness, which they take for a new, unique, noble social conscience, and which is sparsely furnished with a few smug commonplaces pre-fabricated by the mass media and coated with modish pseudo-intellectual Day-Glo paint so that they can pretend to be Ideas and Concepts. The young can't afford to tolerate criticism of either their theory or their practice, nor can they afford to yield to suasion, for their mental equipment is haphazardly constructed on the basis of comic-strip and TV scientology. The paltriness of their argumentation makes them unusually strong and self-assured, like many others who have focused their lamentably limited imagination not on what socialism, democracy, justice, or morality *is* but on what it *could* or *should* be. Some of them speak constantly of all-encompassing compassions and guilts but are frightfully devoid of personal feelings. I have never noticed any of them revealing, during their press-sponsored harangues, the tiniest torment of ambivalence; not one of them, apparently, has ever felt an impulse to mention that in spite of his parents' bourgeois hypocrisy and ugliness he can't help loving them. My generation was spared that malaise of the void because of our agony over a just war that we had to carry on, and then the chore of building a free society. This society was flawed, as everything human is flawed, but at least it eliminated, in its larger segments, the risk of producing an undernourished youth, concerned only with making a living for a living's sake. It saved the youth of today from the abominations of opportunism— an act that eventually proved to be our unforgivable crime in youth's eyes.

THE PROFUNDITIES OF FASHION

In the youthful mind, the political consciousness is hopelessly intertwined with a feeling for fashion. Whole generations feel leftist or rightist because of the vicissitudes of vogue. Leaving aside the political fortunes of the black people in the South and the social fortunes of the blacks elsewhere in the country, hardly anyone could be termed politically oppressed, or repressed, in today's America—the young least of all. But it is extremely fashionable to *feel* politically oppressed. And if a sizable segment of a society thinks itself oppressed, a new reality is created, in which, though no fact of oppression exists, feelings of oppression do exist, and bloom. Popular fashion magazines come closest to sociocognitive discovery when they present models wearing groovy and comfortable dresses for an afternoon protest demonstration or some evening guerilla activity.

CLOTHING AND REVOLUTION

In a society in which the prerevolution revolutionaries proudly dress as revolutionaries, the need for revolution appears questionable.

AMERICAN ANTI-DREAM

Can America be ugly?

Of course. There are more than enough city blocks and other features of existence to prove the hideous, degrading possibilities of the American way of life.

Can American democracy be inhuman and oppressive?

Of course. One has only to peer into some Northern slums and Southern counties; the infamy of all man's subjugations is there, blatantly epitomized.

Can the American social structure be repressive, antiprogressive, and destructive?

Of course. DeTocqueville wrote about the ignominious tyranny of majority opinion, which can have the persecutive power of the Holy Inquisition.

Dissent and rebellion against these elements of Americanism have always been the nature and marrow of Americanism. They were and are deeply ingrained in the American consciousness. A mechanism whose purpose it is to warrant an unhindered defiance is peculiarly American; its intrinsic, privileged presence in American social and political institutions remains the cornerstone of their efficiency. The flexibility and extensibility of this mechanism is infinite—a fact that makes many young Americans think that its total destruction may be the proper solution. They underestimate its absorptive force and its skill at self-preservation. They also ignore the fact that they would become the first victims of its failure.

Today's young are no more and no less American than the prior generations. Americans are always seized by a strange awkwardness in handling their own brand of idealism. They liberate and feed other nations, which subsequently stone American embassies and libraries for not knowing how to be free or to nourish themselves. Idealisms are transmuted according to fleeting imponderables of history, and the current generation of Americans is trying to mold a *new* idealism, imbue it with living content, and make it superior to any earlier one. This is a beautiful attempt, notwithstanding its susceptibility to the same fate as every such attempt before it. A new sensitivity or intensity of emotion is always welcome, but it has to be protected against certain hypocritical smart clichés that can readily abuse and devastate it. If the young manage to improve our social morality and its consequent modes of behavior, they may produce the greatest revolution of our time. Let us not forget, however, that Marx, Lenin, and Guevara tried to do the same thing, with catastrophic results. The young do rebel against plenty of things worth rebelling against, plenty of things that deserve hatred and rejection. But, oddly, even those who observe them most benevolently are not convinced they are right.

Optimism

Actually, a noticeable feature of American democracy is that young simpletons, repeating the most discredited and worn-out slogans and clichés with a potent voice increased by devices of modern mass media, are thoughtfully listened to by the older and wiser. Some observers find it lethal. I think it is optimistic, even cheerful, and an inexhaustible source of perpetual vaudeville.

Volcanology

People who discuss revolution in America generally do not reckon with the obvious fact that revolution has somehow been a constant factor in the American reality since its beginning. It never stopped, only turned, with time into a revolution on the installment plan—which practically denotes every successful evolution. Short periods of relative peacefulness are periodically disrupted by all sorts of unrests whose regular appearance imbues life here with a certain cheerful insouciance about things that could easily bring any other country to the brink of bottomless failure. For someone who doesn't understand this phenomenon, volcanology might be of priceless value. It teaches us that the most disastrous eruptions are those of inactive, somnolent volcanos. The active ones present little danger and generate geysers that make themselves useful in healing rheumatism.

Watch Out For Your Opinions

A famed British sportsman once said in an interview: "You've got to use somebody else's phone system before you realize how lucky you Yanks are."

I try to imagine him pronouncing the same words, just paraphrasing them for a larger simile, before a mildly moderate leftish student gathering on one of the American campuses. Fumes of slaughter hover in my imagination.

THE HOLY PARADOX OF OUR TIME

Utterly bored and exasperated with my equally primitive and stubborn refusal to approve both the ends and the methods of American revolutionaries, a charming and intelligent lady of leftish persuasion said: "We fully understand and sympathize with the upheaval movements behind the Iron Curtain. We feel total empathy with the protest, resistance, and insurgence against Communist tyranny. Our hearts, best wishes, and our sense of justice are ardently with Czech and Polish students, Russian intellectuals, and all those persecuted and oppressed in the Red Empire. Consequently, it is incomprehensible to me why someone like you, who comes from over there, doesn't *want* to understand us, our idealism and revolution, our goals and struggle."

"Madame," I said, "the expression of your eyes seems to me incomparable. I do not even try to look for metaphors. Also your way of using fork and knife appears to me exquisite beyond any comparison."

This brutal deviation from the main subject was my sole escape. The lady was a compleat human being, except for one marginal trait: she didn't know how to respect her freedom. She used to repeat: "But we want to enlarge our freedom, improve it . . ." Unfortunately, this noble intention was, in her opinion, to be implemented by ostracizing and slandering all those who happened to think in a different way. How could my argumentation reach her powers of reason? American revolutionaries are offsprings of a civilization that firmly believes that almost everything should be permitted, for limitation equals repression and impoverishment of human rights. Present East European and Russian revolutionaries rebel against a civilization built upon a principle that almost nothing should be permitted, for confinement enriches a human being and shapes him into a theoretically prescribed ideal. Both civilizations may be equally wrong, but if within the Communist one, the forces of opposition rise logically against a system that makes opposition impossible, their Western counterparts revolt against a system that enables them to revolt. The first ones get killed or sacrifice their personal freedom in order to obtain what the others despise, trample, and want to get rid of without bearing any consequences for their actions. The one yearns desperately for a sociopolitical arrangement that will assure his most basic human dignity, whereas the other, having it, is in the grip of an inexplicable obsession to destroy it and fall down into a limbo of masochistic humiliations among which he expects to reveal, or at least find, new human values. My refined lady with the brilliant mind argues: "It's very natural that the Russians or Czechs want to achieve what we have achieved in primary liberties, output of goods, and their distribution, but *we* have *to move ahead*. We arrived, many years before the others, to a point where freedom is no more freedom, therefore we have to blow up all obstacles that are in our way to new achievements." This is dialectical gabble, simplistic and idealistic as well. The lady speaks from the vantage of someone who was always free and has no idea at all what lack of freedom means. It is like discussing colors with a person born blind. She doesn't know and won't ever know that freedom is indivisible and has no shades or degrees but a oneness that determines its existence. It is or it is not— any attempted variant of that fundamental dichotomy denotes its absence. It is like food—humans can surely live on and be sufficiently fed with substitutes and ersatz pills, but it won't be *food*. The lady and her fellow revolutionaries ignore, or at least want to ignore, Giambattista Vico and all the lessons of history, its circular principle and its theory of spiral progress, or the simple fact that no vacuum is possible in sociopolitical relations. It means that whenever freedom regresses, subjugation and oppression follow. We can still discover new chemical elements, construct an artificial cell, transplant organs, erect a skycraper on planet Venus, and learn about infrastructural depths of psychology, but it is more than doubtful that we shall ever converge and correlate freedom with lack of freedom in one genuine moral value. This is the little, holy paradox of our time, and I have always refused to ponder it at the dinner table.

But perhaps I'm wrong. It may be that improvement is a notion of a higher order than liberty. When I came to this country, I thought New York buses a marvel. Now after three years, I think them overheated in winter, insufficiently air-conditioned in summer, and moronically scheduled. When I've been waiting for a First Avenue bus for half an hour, and then four of them arrive one after another in a row, I'm ready to march on City Hall and execute no matter whom. In Communist Poland, in an analogous situation, I was more than happy if any bus would arrive at all.

Toying With Notions

Youth—which a few years ago appeared on the national scene as a new social class, tending to structure its own civilization, culture, morality, and aesthetics— derives its ideology from the presumption that only newly created values and criteria are valid, *de rigueur*, and worthy of being projected into the future. Benefiting from the education and erudition provided by their elders, youth formulates its analysis and thesis in full contempt for the past, principally for the so-called timeless imponderabilia that constitute the intellectual treasure and emotional muscle of all who do not belong to youth. Thus, avoiding conflict is all but impossible.

The conflict is unusually acrimonious not because we don't try, or agree to try, to understand each other, but because—perhaps for the first time in history—we're actually unable to understand each other. Being loyal to my generation, I feel in full accord with myself in accusing youth unilaterally. They are guilty, not we. Their current password is improvement, but they do not really want any improvement as such. They want us to concede that they invented improvement as a notion, which is not true. From the dawn of mankind, *homo* mastered the device of improvement, both in the cognitive as well as in the empirical sense. During our stay on this planet, we have improved plenty of things around us, and even a few things in us. My generation was as busy at improving as any other, and we won't ever agree to let ourselves be deprived of what we hold to be the content of our lives. What makes the current young generation so blindly conceited as to claim the invention of something that always existed?

IGNORANCE AND TABOOS

People used to say: the young are always right, time and history give them that credit. They represent the inevitable future, and are charismatic bearers and heralds of an unavoidable truth.

These assertions are false. If we only dare doubt them, they easily turn from the axiomatic to the ridiculous. Youth is sometimes right and sometimes wrong, and history is replete with facts to prove the second eventuality. One has only to study it. A nonsensical belief that youth has a special mission to fulfill and is endowed with exceptional perceptiveness stems from the period of the *Sturm und Drang,* Johann Gottlieb Fichte, German Romanticism, and its philosophy that in the end led to Nazism.

Producing taboos out of ignorance is as old as limestone, but neither the producers nor helplessly worshipping customers are able to admit it, and stubbornly proclaim each current taboo as the last word in the human spirit of innovation and progress. Of late, the most oppressive taboo, apologetically idolized by many, is that everything should be permitted. If everything is to be permitted, then the most rational and justified prohibition turns into abuse that distorts human character and condones resistance. Art and theatre critics are, in our epoch, unusually busy fabricating and defending some of the most ludicrous taboos. They claim, for instance, that everything is permitted in terms of content and form and consequently wonder why everything around them seems to be so trashy. Having no real value to praise, they elevate artful gimmicks to various pantheons; and by blundering in the maze of their own errors, they have no other choice but to mystify orders and qualities. Which is nothing else than tinkering with taboos.

WORLD & CHANGE

Does the world change? Of course, but it changes less than it does not change, even if it is pushed by force.

The youth, judging from appearances, and taking pushing for change itself, believes in the reverse. This gloomy evidence underlies our trouble. It has been always this way, proving best the limited potency of change.

AMERICA & CHANGE

The password "change" has lately acquired quite a mystical significance. I think we have reached a point where America, always prone to rapid change, has to worry more about what to _preserve_ and _protect_ than what to change. From its beginning, America has traditionally taken pride in its swift replacement of goods and values with constantly newer goods and values. This swiftness has sometimes been rather embarrassing, proving that the young American civilization tends to forget that aging is _not_ an ultimate negative, that things and contents have a strange facility for reappearing on life's scene, and that accumulation of time may reveal itself as an enormous value both in the spiritual as well as in the material sense. The American way of disintegrating things is so fast that it induces an almost immediate disintegration of substance, consequently bringing with it an infinitely more dangerous disintegration of values.

The last two hundred years of culture have been permeated with a popular unwillingness to admit that the preserved values and cultural motives were more powerful and creative than elements of change. Honest research could rectify many obsolete judgments The endless search for the new somehow seems vulgar to me, but it's a strictly personal view. I have always preferred an old chair, overcoat, church, and well-experienced principle to new ones. I wonder why all those who ceaselessly want something new don't understand that "new" is a concept from the realm of toys. The Pyramids and the computer, printing and the H-bomb are mankind's toys, some of them dangerous and lethal. In spite of their superb complexity and marvelous nature, they have proven completely unable to remove from our shoulders even the slightest burden of disappointment or the unattainable. The struggle with passing time seems one of the most admirable features of humanness. An effort to overcome time and remain useful, beautiful, and wise becomes a glory and a pride. Of course, it may also only attest to my progressing immobilization and petrifaction.

ETERNITIES

I was passing next to a swelling group, young and excited, that apparently was trying to transform itself into a manifestation. Placards were hastily fixed and arranged, covered with familiar nouns and verbs. They expressed the same arrogant and belligerent multivocality that is as instrumental in dividing people as it is in bringing them together. A couple attracted my attention; they were a classic embodiment of the idea, painted and tattooed, decorated with all sorts of beads, dressed in a mixture of pseudo-oriental vanity with aggressive Cuban-Bolshevik overtones. Both were pale, not too well scrubbed and visibly exhausted from starvation or ideology. She carried a baby in her arms. The infant, dismayed or annoyed by the crowd, started to scream. The girl tried to calm it with gentle words and hugging but unsuccessfully. Then she began lulling. It was the same lulling movement of the female body my mother used to do with me, and my grandmother surely applied to my mother, and probably Eve used when she wanted to appease the exasperated Cain. I felt a little embarrassed. I didn't think of it before, but I presume I always took it for granted that the rebels would hold it beneath them to use such a traditional method. At the same time, however, my ever-present anxiety about mankind's future was dissipating. "How wonderful," I thought, "if someone, let's say a Supreme Intelligence, could take the whole group on His lap and cuddle them fondly. Maybe that is what they really need."

THE MELANCHOLY OF A DOUBLE STANDARD

Whenever there is a confrontation, the attackers against order are called by the American press "kids," and the defenders of the order are labeled as "police," "men," or "an overreacting force." Outlandish convergences of myths and reality result from that calcified nomenclature. When the Yippies—members of the Youth International Party—invaded such a venerable landmark of the New York sentimental *paysage* as Grand Central Station, and tried to convert it into their ideal of joyful and liberated nonfunctioning, they were cleared away by members of the city's Tactical Patrol Force—a special police unit created to handle more complicated cases of disorder. Now the average age of the Yippies, according to my private research, is about 22 years, with their leadership reaching a masculine 30. The average age of the T.P.F. policemen is 24 years, and many of them pursue a college education in their off-duty time. However, it has to be added that an average Yippie, in conformity with his openly professed faith, has exhausted nearly every possibility in sex, drugs, and the dissipation of morality, erstwhile called sin or vice, and his general life experience resembles that of an old rake from a century ago. On the other hand a T.P.F. policeman's life, compared to that of a Yippie, looks like an embarrassing model of medieval adolescence, in order to live up to the police code of conduct and police-hiring standards. The Yippie, when it comes to abuses of mores, claims the same rights as those of a worn-out lovelace; but when prohibited from outrageous behavior, he screams that he is a *kid*. In the meantime, the T.P.F. policeman considers himself a *man*, both in his duties, as well as in his privileges. What seems most astonishing is the position taken by the American press—in the aftermath of the Grand Central battle, it stubbornly insisted on contrasting the Yippies as spirited *kids* and the T.P.F. people as dull, intolerant *men*. It should be noticed, however, that the American press considers itself the most perceptive and impartial in the world.

The American Press's Sense of Responsibility

We face now a more dangerous issue than that of the student rebellion. It's the high school revolt. The lower we descend, the more the complicated, brittle, and perilous elements emerge, as the margin of rational approach to responsibility shrinks in quite a surrealistic way. The natural youthful belligerence, boisterousness, and rambunctiousness, endowed with pseudopolitico-ideological argument and overtones, leads to a nightmarish, absurb buffoonery, and ends with petty tragedies of mugged and knifed teachers. The role the American information media play in this phenomenon is a little hideous. The so-called objective exposure becomes a display of staggering mindlessness. *The New York Times*, that bastion of American journalistic seriousness and correctness, carried a story about a teen-age, high school militant whose pretended "political" enunciation indicated an acute case of *dementia praecox*. The title of the story: "——(name of the boy) is organizing a revolution against American society with the skill of a little Lenin." If this is what's meant by responsibility for the word, and the mature recognition of its consequences, I shudder to think what irresponsibility may be.

The Princeton Tales

Not long ago in Princeton—the site of a famous university—the Americans convoked a strange gathering. They invited scientists and intellectuals from all around the world to express themselves about America, its drawbacks, limitations, errors, backwardness, ineptitude, and lack of skill in handling everything from world politics to cuisine. Of course, the invited Frenchmen, Britons, Greeks, and Eastern Europeans accepted the invitation with suspicious alacrity, got free air tickets, luxurious accomodations, and even better board, and started to pour buckets of hogwash on America with such an eagerness that it aroused some doubts even among the courteous, attentive Americans who wanted to learn something from their European colleagues through knowledgeable impartiality and objectivity. One of them remarked that perhaps it would have been advisable if representatives of nations that unleashed two world wars, lost huge empires, and that have been unable to manage their own economies, had shown a little more restraint and modesty in criticizing and condemning. But this sheepish reflection only increased the scoffers' fervor. If someone in Communist Eastern Europe conceived the idea for a similar convocation, he would be put in jail for life. The French and British would probably execute anyone who dared call into question their all-encompassing superiority and betterness and claim, at the same time, free meals and hotel accommodations. But in America the superstitious esteem for everything foreign has deep roots in tradition, derived from a nostalgic idealization of the "old country," where everything was better except personal poverty or oppression. It is fully reflected in American literature, and later in the movies, where an Eastern sage, a Russian maestro, an English aristocrat, a Hungarian violinist, an Austrian doctor, a German scientist, and a French perfumer were *a priori* considered as commanding a pious reverence attributed to those whose superiority constituted a dogma. I know a case of a professor from Eastern Europe with a strong financial nerve who invented a simple but lucrative gimmick—he tells his students that everything in Europe within his discipline is better than in America. The American universities pay him large amounts of money for his deep insight into the matter.

A Fantasy to Come

The American force of pervasion is so immense that it often results in corrupting Evil—with all due reservation about the relativity of what is bad. Supersquare executives purchasing at Madison Avenue stores beads and amulets, initially conceived as exorcistic equipment against them, and sporting them at their suburban dinner parties, are only one example that stimulates reflection. This ambivalent power of corruption opens perspectives that might have endowed the American civilization with a Messianic thrust. We can duly assume that even the most righteous and principled anticapitalist revolution here would become, in a short time, an inexhaustible source of income and healthy, constructive buildup of investment and industrial output. Let's take barricades, for instance. Couldn't they be prepared in advance, in an appropriate variety of sizes, styles, shapes, and versions—the ready-made, prefabricated, frozen, or make-it-yourself kind, with French, Spanish, Congo, or Indonesian ornamentation—individual, family-size, for couples only, or for larger congregations? Not to mention smaller outfits, Molotov cocktails with factional New Left mix, or modish rebel caps from all epochs . . . .

Pure Americana

Neither the cowboy hat, nor the hot dog stand, nor the "Chapel in the Moonlight" represent the pure American phenomena of today, but social dadaism, a radical movement without any popular roots and a new snobbery as a historic force. Dadaistic political sermons make the folklore of this country. Everyone refers to the American people, but what are the American people? The people of wealthy workers? The American working class—or, more classically, the proletariat—evidently turned, in the last two decades, into a classic middle-class syndrome. It constitutes now the only middle-class in history that cannot be reproached for *not* being a proletariat. Along with the Marxist dogma, it is dispossessed of the means of production, but its countless members own stock. What a fine field for an interplay of all kinds of snobbery, misplaced allegiances, biased hatreds, and ridiculous adulations!

AMERICAN CENTURY

Opinions are to be heard voicing a despondent note about America's disappointing historical performance and consequential decline. America haters, both outside and inside the country, outdo one another in gloomy predictions and preach America's inevitable failure. One of them, a distinguished Britisher, exclaimed not without *Schadenfreude:* "This is not going to be the American century. Very few people are enamored of the American way of life."

The gentleman is perfectly right when doubting the future. It has no need to be, because it already *is* an American century, and almost from its beginning. It became American not because of cohorts and legions, nor for anything that rules the waves, nor by exporting homemade revolution, but because of a glorious share in the two most important wars of liberation mankind has experienced, and the unheard-of attitude of the principal winner who didn't annex one single inch of the soil of his defeated foes. Neither tanks, nor cannons and an ever-readiness to use them, nor even an unlimited, never-seen-before economic magnitude denote an American century, but an unprecedented civilizational impact and influence upon the rest of humanity. Hence the gentleman's grave error, and to check how wrong he is, he has but to look around his native England and recognize how Americanized it has become during the last twenty-five years, how many American words have become indispensable in his native language, and how many people from London, Glasgow, and Dublin would prefer and opt for the American way of life. An argument that America is richer and pays better wages has no value, for if a country is more affluent and rewards better those who work for it, it testifies only to its superiority, which, if achieved not by conquest, must have stemmed from the skills and qualities of its people and its institutions. However, resourcefulness and industriousness would not explain the obvious phenomenon that few places exist on this planet where little boys do not play cowboys, and bigger boys do not sing rock 'n' roll, where the word "Hollywood" has never been pronounced, "Star Dust" hummed, and the New York skyline seen either on a screen or in illustrations. No one forces humanity to watch American movies, listen to American music, dance American dances, read American books, and wear American clothes; nonetheless, all over the world these products of American civilization are best-selling items. If the gentleman only knew with what piety some Europeans listen today to a ragtime tune long forgotten in America, how oriented they are in American history, with what a fanatical curiosity they leaf through old American illustrated magazines, he probably could understand *what* "American Century" means.

In the Communist empire, as a matter of fact, people are inhibited and persecuted for their craving for Americanism, which only increases their avidity, endows everything American with a charisma, and makes names like Max Factor, Coca Cola, and William Faulkner more full of content than the names of Lenin, Socialism, and Sholokhov. Charlie Chaplin's California and Gary Cooper's Wild West became the most romantic landscapes for several generations on five continents, and countless millions

melt in tears at the end of "West Side Story," although
no one sheds any anymore when they reach the end of
"Romeo and Juliet," which, as Monsieur de Talleyrand
once said: "I don't say it's good, I don't say it's bad, I say
it's the way it is."

For me, the notion "American Century" bears a deeper
sense. We are now witnessing a strange exodus from
Communist-dominated Eastern Europe. People are fleeing
inconspicuously, but almost massively, the martyred
Czechoslovakia, Poland in a neo-Nazi grip, and lethargic
Hungary. Many of them could find better opportunities
on other continents that are ready to provide them with
infinitely better material opportunities than the daily
hardship of American competition. The highest-priced
win though, a prize on life's lottery, is considered a free
entry to the U. S. One can find among them political ras-
cals whose last twenty-five years were devoted to be-
smirching America and its institutions, to lying about it,
to slandering and hating it according to the most insolent
and obscurantist Communist gospel. For all that, they
come here looking for refuge.

This circumstance of providing enemies with shelter
shines through the moral darkness enveloping our epoch
and gives to it more than anything else the title "American."

CONFESSION

When young, I hated oppressors, persecutors, and
invaders. With the years, hatred turned into melancholic
scorn. Today I find it difficult to hate anything—except
conformism disguised as nonconformism.

ON PERSONAL SYMPATHIES

"Why don't you openly admit," a young, radical
student said, "that you don't like revolutionaries."

"Certainly," I admitted, "I don't like them indeed. Human experience, collected through centuries, teaches us that the more ardent a revolutionary, the easier he turns into a ruthless, self-appointed policeman. Policemen have to be hired. Only the hired ones can be fired. Sometime ago I saw one of those superbly shallow French movies that pretend to know everything with not one single streak of incertitude. The film was a compilation of diverse emotions, psychic conditions, and concrete facts taken from the life of an aging Spanish revolutionary in exile. He was the embodiment of the ethical norms of the world's New Left psychological penchants, gusto, longings, predilections and snobberies, and represented its archetype, ideal, and apotheosis. The man was handsome, well dressed, utterly tired (he had fought against fascism), frustrated (he hadn't defeated it), embittered, contemptuous, had sexual intercourse during the movie with two ladies—substantially differentiated in looks and age—and above all, he continued combating and subverting Franco, an activity that he found virtuous and just as exciting. For me, however, the movie was cluttered with future follow-ups, and I could easily imagine what would become of the protagonist after his victory. I saw too many of his kin in Eastern Europe, also Spanish revolutionaries. With astounding facility, they skipped from their romantic countenances to the most callous and blood-thirsty secret police activity, changing into cruel henchmen, and hunting and torturing all those who were at odds with their Communist revolution. In hoary Europe we have known by heart some political peculiarities that seem unimaginable to young Americans, for example, the perennial and weird partnership between all the New Lefts in history and the perpetual Old Totalitarianism. When the extreme Right wins, many leftish intellectuals transmogrify miraculously into its faithful servants, fascinated by brutal, victorious strength, and digging out some neurotic delights from their abasement. When the extreme Left wins, the rightist thugs form its muscle, enlist massively, and get jobs in the political police."

"It's a long time," snapped my collocutor, "since I have heard arguments based on so much personal prejudice."

"I know," I sighed, feeling contrite. "No one finds them convincing. Except those who saw the revolutionaries *after* a revolution."

A PRETENDED WORD FROM W.S.

Never in any time could Caliban feel more *à l'aise* than among the intellectual rebels of our era. He would be socially accepted, adored by party-goers, an authority on hairdos and environmental conflict, and praised by subtle social critics for his best-selling, seminal manuals of moral behavior.

OUR POOR VICTIMIZED EGO

There is a universal outcry about our lost identity. We seem to be submerging ourselves in a sociocosmic catastrophe of alienation, anonymity, and loss of personal features. We are sentenced to dissolve in an apocalyptic, mystical entity called inventively the "nameless, faceless crowd." The destiny of today's man is to be on the side-lines tossing acclaim to others. As an American writer put it not long ago—he's got to be a fan. The depersonalized world of our time generates in its womb a giant revolution against depersonalization.

A few questions arise. When was man's identity a social, economic, political, or historical issue? Whenever the world wasn't replete with anonymous creatures standing facelessly along the paths of history and, according to circumstances, booing or cheering the others. Mankind, since its dawn, has been composed of namelessness, idleness, and an effort to overcome both—with its elemental, single, anonymous, and humble components timelessly and devouringly watching either the gladiators or Popes, or TV. The point is that *he* did not always feel nameless or devoid of identity, as some maintain he feels now. And if he does, I doubt that it's only TV to blame.

GUILT

A sociology professor told me the following story: "When researching in Brooklyn, I came across and interviewed an old man in the vicinity of Bedford Avenue. He was a Hassidic Jew who had survived Hitler's concentration camp and had come here after the last war. He said to me: 'My son, a student, arrives home each evening from his college and begins a discussion with me. He challenges my spiritual peacefulness. He bids for my penitence which appears to me totally incomprehensible. He calls on me to feel guilty for the Negro plight of the last four centuries. I answer him that my whole family was bestially murdered, and I myself was forced to sleep in excrement and deprived of the rest of humanness by my torturers. He says that this is the past and has no more significance today. Then I say that I can't have any feeling of guilt for something that happened four centuries ago, and neither I nor any of my ancestors from Byelorussia had taken part in it. He says that I am a wanton adherent of the corporate industrial-military complex. If he has in mind General Patton and his troops who liberated people from Dachau and Buchenwald, I must proudly admit that I am . . . .' "

ASSORTED WORRIES

We have entered an age of insincerity and phoniness, all but impossible to detect. Sophisticated labels are invented: *Umwertung aller Werte,* or "Disintegration of Contents." As a matter of fact, values and notions do not break down or perish. They get distorted, deformed, and degraded, the process of annihilation affects only what's sensitive and can get easily biased. But whatever is tackled becomes tangled, and consequently it loses its perennial usefulness in moral and social service.

The prophets of the *in* revolution claim that man, frightened by impersonality and the anonymity of existence, must revolt. But who feels that way? Certainly not the poor and underprivileged in this country. They crave for much simpler delights than meaningfulness and structural identity. Social climbing and its material confirmation are enough for them. They neither feel bored by opulence, nor call trouble alienation, nor get frustrated by nuances of success. According to Lenin, fear, frustration, and decadence have always distinguished the outgoing classes, defending their doomed order. If he lived in today's America, his clearcut analysis would be blurred. If he wanted to remain brilliant and accurate, he should have added lines about revolution as the pastime for the rich, or the opiate for the affluent and their children.

The *jeunesse dorée* was always counterrevolutionary, although an infinite number of good-family offspring had tuned in on countless revolutions. Many bright individuals of aristocratic or middle-class descent have helped to organize, shape, and carry out revolutions against their own classes. Never in history, however, has a whole stratum of middle-class progeny, wealthy and enraged as well, become a *sole* incubator of revolt against matters fatally intertwined with their ideals of thought and behavior. Lenin, of course, would recognize a suicidal trend in it, but perhaps, he would not be believed this time. All the same, what name do you give to a call to action by those not oppressed who do not defend anything that actually needs defense? Don't they understand that all the poignancy and validity of their protest is profoundly and indissolubly interwoven with this country's established values and the sociopolitical mechanism they are trying to destroy? What do they challenge? An order that takes pride in encouraging challenge? Which lack of virtue is revamped again and attributed an awesome consideration as a new virtue? "Our word is action!" proclaim the young, proud of their spirit of inventiveness. We, who grew up in the thirties, can only smile sadly. We know what it means. For us that is fascism. The Nazi ideology emphasized action as an objective and autonomous value, and we know where it led. I remember the ravaged Jewish homes and massacred Jewish people whose agony was caused by that sacred word. When a minority wants to impose its will upon a majority, the vocable "action" acquires some mystic gaiety and innocence. Its only sequel is dismal, monstrous injustice, also called tyranny.

A catastrophist would draw an unequivocal conclusion —everything in human hands falls asunder and decays. Our good intention is our doom to come. Psychoanalysis has attempted to improve us; better understanding was supposed to make better men out of our children. It ended with chaotic permissiveness and the neo-idolatry of spurious values. Our fake sublimation and suspiciously overzealous care for characters and egos of entire generations brought about distrust, disenchantment and appalling bitterness of an intensity that outdoes any boundaries of logical concern. Our penetrating preoccupation with the spiritual and ontological health of our future fellowmen has resulted in a cry for revolution from those who were never hungry, who never worked for their living, who never built, sowed, or harvested anything. Our jealous quest for liberal impartiality and understanding, and our intransigent worship of free expression, has led us face to face with the hopeless abuse of the word, and with those who say: "Our country is *always* wrong!" although they *never* contributed to any good in it.

Being an optimist, I think that if they haven't, it's because they haven't had enough time to do it yet.

To Restructure

The verb "to restructure" is on its way to becoming an important, notionwise, semantic figure in the near future. It's already quite fashionable and instrumental in urban semiphilosophical debates. Like every chic word, it contains as much nonsense as euphemism, unless this is not considered a paradox. Many are prone to overlook that structure used to be the only categorical and intangible element of an edifice. Isn't it simpler to operate with a less appealing verb like "to demolish?"

On Communication

If the medium is the message, we are hopelessly disconnected. Communication is out. Even an exchange of ideas may be very doubtful when words and notions are losing their common value. "Freedom," "happiness," "objectivity," "tolerance," "love," "sense," "purpose," "guilt" —among many others—already mean something different for the young and for us. Contention over anonymity is archetypal. People who think anonymity not an individual and psychological but rather, a social and political problem, related to all sorts of administrative strife, are in fact from another galaxy. It becomes almost impossible to detect whether by saying "lack of identity" they do not mean "lack of influence," or if "meaningfulness" doesn't equal "domineering" and "prevailing" in their minds.

Not everything is lost, however. "Disease," "death," "impossibility," "defeat," "frustration" have strangely the same sense for them as for us. Even if some of them insist that we cannot communicate in these matters, let's just wait a few years.

COMPLEXITIES OF TRANSPORTATION

If someone boarded an airy, convenient, and punctual bus, on which we were just being comfortably transported, and started having words with the driver accusing him of the felonious lack of a flowerbed of daffodils in the middle of the vehicle, we would be legitimately vexed. We would properly consider the person troublesome and a little out of his mind. But if some student demands at American universities present inadequate logic and factual value, many reflect on them carefully and are uncertain of what to say or do. They often explain that the bus is in fact not perfect and might be substantially bettered —which is very true, for even the best bus can still evolve into a better one, according to the nature of things. It's dubious, however, if blocking passage by planting some charming weeds would enhance anything in a bus that, after all, is quite easy to distinguish from a garden. After all, a university, as someone pointed out, is a place where those who know less come to get something from those who know more; and there is little chance of substituting this old, banal, overlooked, and unattractive truth with anything more appealing. Of late, students want to determine what they should know. How they know what they should know, being unknowledgeable seekers of knowledge, remains a mystery. Discussing it brings all of us to a stage of toddling.

MISANTHROPY?

I don't want to sound misanthropic, but I must admit that, as far as I'm concerned, everyone under thirty seems to me a deadly bore. It's a real drag to listen to their utterly banal discoveries, which they think are revelations and which so many before them have rejected as insupportable junk. It's lamentably dull to be exposed to their cumbersome torments full of the most suspect and treacherous moral *kitsch* they proclaim as unshakable truth and commandment. So few of them escape being tedious by being polite and having truly their own opinions.

MORAL SANITY

Man's crucial problem at present is how to deal with his own power of procreating and preserving life. Organization is the key to our future. It is becoming more complex and oppressive with each new billion of people on the planet. With the earth's population multiplying beyond any sensibility, humanity's big question is how to live together. If we do not organize, our immensity will crumble us, we will suffocate under our own weight, and smother in our madly-increasing inability to perform functions. If we do not establish a system of complex cooperation, we will perish. Very different notions of social interdependence have to emerge, and the world has to accept them if it doesn't want to retrogress to unheard-of cruelty, the decay of the most valuable human instincts, and the practical end of the anthropocentric civilization. The childish grumbling of the common burgher against the increasing role of bureaucracy becomes an elaborate philosophical rumination concerning life's depersonalization, the neomystical power concept, and dehumanized superstructures disposing of individual destinies. Now, once more, America steps to the front of the stage. With its multitude of diverse conflicts and galactic variety of issues, obsessed by a devouring passion for solving anything that seems insoluble, America becomes a lighthouse in the darkness of a century already known for its unsurpassed mechanization of murder. And it offers two antagonistic answers.

One outlines the inevitable necessity to organize *with-*

out losing the sacrosanct sense of individual and social freedom. The other is simpler and advises a revolution in order to destroy the existing state of things. Its partisans, when asked what about after the revolution, are usually unable to propose anything that hasn't been checked out yet by mankind, proven unbearable, and rejected as unfit. Thus, reckoning on its help with the future becomes farcical. Noticing that their suggestions contain little relevance to our epoch's crucial problems, they answer that it can be mastered by building up, imposing, and organizing another superstructure which *a priori* has to be much superior to the one destroyed because they are going to construct it. Some of them feel more responsible to common sense and advocate socialism. But Marxian socialism has lost its chance for delivering any appealing answer. Fifty years of the Communist agglomeration of failures and crimes, committed in the name of socialism, has removed the possibility of any hope from that direction.

All American liberties are founded upon the sage principle that people differ in every respect. Reality is composed of a countless variety of species and elements, insomuch that the only way to preserve a healthy society is to accept and observe the otherness of the other. This is also called pluralism. How it may work under the pressure of overpopulation, we don't know. However, if we only exchange a few words and say: to accept and observe the otherness of the alike, we discover a transposed sense which may prove viable, even priceless, in the oncoming condition. It may sanction that moral sanity that we need to survive. For so-called moral insanity, inherent in so many human ideas and deeds, is enough discredited with the help of history, science, the invention of print, movies, and even TV, that it's wiser to be a little afraid of it.

Maoism

At a party, I met a young man with a frail Victorian face, so often found in Massachusetts post offices, who was busy explaining to me his devotion to the Maoist cause. I asked him if he could produce what he considered the finest sample of the little Red Book's wisdom. He quoted a verse of such improbable platitudes and pompous, commonplace, truistic character that I was gripped by sudden fright. Are we slowly being engulfed by monumental idiocy? And what is worse: to drown in an ocean of churlishness and cruelty, or to be swept away by sanctified and institutionalized imbecility?

Law

Through the ages, law has been the best deterrent against human licentiousness, also called crime. Laws can be limitlessly improved, but it's dubious whether the principle of law as the chief instrument of communal existence can be any better. In recent decades America has been experimenting with the very notion of law, trying to replace it with some sociopsychological components of the human condition. It was a proud attempt to demonstrate that there is less injustice in America than anywhere in the world. The results, however, turned out to be rather meager. Americans, in their vanity tend sometimes to forget that there is as much suffering and injustice in America as everywhere else where the human condition produces it, which puts no blame on America, of course, but on the human condition.

America Incredible

Puerto Ricans riot in New York. It takes three days to calm them. People are injured and arrested, and there is property damage all around. During the peace talks that follow, Puerto Rican leaders explain the cause of the unrest—their people feel that the New York police, by the mere fact of patroling the streets and being present and seen, invade their sense of privacy. The mayor of New York and high police officials take their places at the conference table, and negotiations, in all seriousness, go on.

IDEOLOGY

There are people around us who proclaim revolution in a society where an overwhelming majority is quite happy with and indeed may even relish the existing social *status quo*. They seem to forget the difference between a revolution and a *mise-en-scène* of a revolution. The latter requires just a bunch of passionate devotees and ambitious daredevils with a high school education, and it usually turns into a minor riot. The former, if within the standards of sensibility, must meet the demands, approval and acceptance—conscious or unconscious, total or partial—of a large mass of people. If not, it easily changes from sublime loftiness into ugly tragedy.

In a democracy, any preparation of the revolutionary stage setting, both theoretical and practical is permitted and goes on in the open, whereas in a totalitarian state, the revolutionary-to-be performers are physically exterminated before they affect the pose. But one should never confound a stage set, even a most expressive one, with real life. Every child who was once in a theatre gets a feeling for it.

A human awareness that is cut off from the cause-and-effect scheme is an inferior one. Many political movements of today appear to operate on, that sort of brainwashed, simplistic mental order—no matter what was before, what the reasons for action, or what the results are going to be. Whereas the only legitimate cause for revolution, as well as its sole guarantee of success,

is an inability to satisfy the needs of the social majority—
either spiritual or material or both. Any other reason may
justify only a *putsch* or a *coup-d'état* which, in Western
civilization, exude a traditionally bad smell. In spite of all
its unprepossessing defects, the democratic capitalism of
our century has revealed itself more than capable of
satisfying not only material needs, but also the psychological whims of overwhelming segments of the population. Some accuse it of creating needs, but what's wrong
with creating desires that are consistently and dutifully
satisfied?

The democratic capitalism of our time means an enormous community that thinks, endeavors, works, and
strains to fulfill the needs of human beings. It is said that
the greed for profit motivates its dynamic activities. What
does it matter? The directive to answer needs remains the
only important thing. Watching it in America, where it is
implemented in a fascinating way, may become one's life
purpose. Some scientists assert that the age of ideology
is over, and there are many proofs that they are right.
But actually, meeting and fulfilling human needs *is* still
an ideology. And how compelling it is to observe an
ideology taking physical shape without ruining lives,
breaking bones and consciences, or establishing concentration camps. What a spectacle!

CHINESE WISDOM

I don't think our epoch is stupider or more senseless and violent than any other. I don't think we face more
insidious problems and venture into more precarious issues than other men did. I think our time is an interesting
one. And there is an old Chinese curse that says: "May
God let you live in an interesting time! . . ."

7.

Revolution In West and East:

Comparative Notes On Two Implausibilities

GENERAL

History, partitioned into epochs, tends to exhibit two general tendencies. Periods when human perfection is pursued and elevated to an acme among values are followed by others when idolatry of productivity and solid accomplishment in marble, steel, and concrete, conquers human souls. From time to time, a third trend prevails—that of giddy worship of existence's sensual delights. Of course, each of these philosophies only seldom monopolizes the historic scene. They often merge in various proportions. But it happens sometimes that they conflict. Then, mankind gets confused, issues become hopelessly obscured, and people start talking about revolution as the sole remedy. Usually, they do not know what they are talking about.

PARTICULAR

I have been asked: "Basically, do you accept an eventuality of violent change frequently called revolution?"

I knew no answer, feeling numbed by the bewildering number of questions I would have to ask before I could have replied, so I said: "It depends." But the next morning, while shaving, it came to my mind that *basically* I don't know whether I would be able to accept revolution, and will *never* know. It also occurred to me that the morning shave appears to be the most intellectually prolific part of the day. I remembered a charming columnist in Poland who once used to run a cute weekly column under a heading: "Thinking during a shave." In a Communist country, such a heading connotes loitering and procrastination, but also a sort of independence, and— needless to say—a pleasure with a dash of proud scepticism. But in an industrial-democratic society shaving never attained that status, habitually being considered a waste of time and therefore reduced to few hasty gestures. Musing on revolution when shaving, however, somehow restores the latter's splendor. After all, a razor and blade are ideal for conveying certain ideas.

NOMENCLATURES

An extraordinary situation emerged: in two parts of the world two forceful groups of remarkable intensity, characterized by young age and revolutionary zeal, try to reach two different goals using the same words. Both proclaim mutual solidarity, empathy, and understanding; both believe in conceptual exactitude of their terminologies; both pledge allegiance to the same ideals. The more they solemnly swear to the identity of their ends, the further they drift apart and fail to communicate when life brings them face to face.

RULE

By saying: American revolutionary—I focus on a person young enough to be honest and self-satisfied, naive and omniscient, emotional and intolerant. He rejects codified moralities and substitutes for them idealistic leanings that frequently rectify their gist from one morning to another. He says: "To hell with reason and order when people get killed or go hungry!" And he looks impatiently around for rationalizations of what he has said. He is overcome by rage, which he calls constructive, but which proves only that he's good at heart. He repels the slightest presumption that life might be composed of discrepancies; this brings him to an insouciant denying of freedom to those who would never deny it to him, and he would feel hurt if someone were to brand it as indecent because he *is* decent. He thinks, in all his integrity, that only social systems and human abjectness are to blame for human misery and all that has to be done to improve the world is to shatter them into shreds. His fair and dynamic longing for a better quality of life, usually labeled militancy or activism, often gets abused and manipulated by acrid revolutionary bigots and technicians whose only dream is enforcing an implementation of their ideas.

By saying: Eastern European or young Russian revolutionary—I have in mind a student or young intellectual who fights for the betterment of his social condition, which he often identifies with human dignity. He is lonely, in most cases separated from any support from those who think similarly, surrounded by fright and mistrust. His ideological armor he can get solely from himself. So, too, any supply of arguments and hope, tenets and faith. His ends are simple: Order through Reason and Freedom for everybody. This constructive modesty of demands makes them insupportably circumspect by Western standards. The silent acclaim of his society is his only reward for his single-handed defiance of an authority notorious for its cruelty, brutality, and insidiousness. For his defiance he has to pay a price, the true sense and weight of which is impossible to transmit to his American brother. Obviously, oppression and persecution cannot be scaled. Neither their shade nor amount make any difference. No matter how measured, they always remain just oppression and persecution—the malediction of humanity. But the impotence of appraising the proportions of respective suffering makes any comparative process a bit futile.

SADNESS

To know what freedom and democracy is, an Eastern European rebel will have to live to see it.

An American revolutionary will acquire a knowledge of the same after democracy and freedom cease to exist here. Now, their presence obscure their sense, significance, and importance. Sadly enough, their lack reveals their value. They generate fierce devotion after they have gone.

FACTS

In our time, actually, revolution is quite impossible in:

—a genuinely democratic country where a majority doesn't wish a revolution;

—in a modern totalitarian state equipped with all the up-to-date devices of modern totalitarian rule—from electronics to the manipulation of the masses theory.

Thus, our further divagations have no practical purpose and can be envisaged only as an engaging dialectical frolic.

RAPPORT

What unifies an American with an Eastern European revolutionary is their mutual ignorance. Outwardly, they pledge reciprocality in admiration and eagerly exchange slogans about their solidarity or declarations of loyalty. When it comes to goals and enemies, it's then that the false tone foists itself in. One of them fights a viable and energetic democracy, whereas the other wrestles a robust and brutal totalitarianism. It results in a rift so deep that even the fiendish deviousness of the two imperialistic establishments cannot serve as explanation for its bottomlessness. Mutual disdain and disbelief, although sedulously concealed, hover about. The socioeconomic predicament of his Eastern European counterpart is the flimsiest of notions for an American; his knowledge of the political scene poorly superficial. An Eastern European knows more about America, but is prone to endless simplification under the pressure of his plight. For the American, confrontation means life; for the other, death—at least a civil one. The American accuses the Eastern European bitterly of *petit bourgeois* ideals and ends. The Eastern European calls the American a zany.

SINCERITY & TRADITION

The American rebel is an heir to the proudest revolutionary tradition in history. He inherits a dialectically and emotionally sanctified promulgation that Everything Is Possible And Feasible. Armed with such a tenet, he rejects the forces of reason and relativity, thus determining both his strength and gullibility. His ultimate court of appeal remains, therefore, his conscience—one of the most slippery and unreliable weapons in man's perennial fight against his own imperfection. "Down with experience, complexity, knowledge, and history!"—is the current battlecry of the American, who stubbornly refuses to acknowledge the fact that his hastily adopted prophets have founded their careers on the careful studies of history, complexity, and experience. His are eruptions of lugubrious candor which he only considers an all-redeeming virtue, a new message, and a flicker of hope on the horizon of human expectations. Sincerity always was, and still is, quite praiseworthy. Nonetheless, it's hard to recognize an universally-craved and mass-modeled salvation in it. Thus, sultrily desired success for universality of appeal and response is—and probably will be forever—denied to the American revolutionary.

An Eastern European rebel is complex, kinky, and insincere. His survival depends on his talent to make believe, and on his evasiveness. Candor is as low in price in his theory as in his practice. Even at the moment of open confrontation, he strenuously flinches from uncontrolled publicity and is oddly superstitious about being photographed or otherwise perpetuated by mass media. He knows that cameras may be more dangerous than guns—he cares for his family and friends, who, in years to come, may have been handicapped by the instant outburst of his political fortunes. He is neither adventurous nor pugnacious, but he is heroic—as everyone besieged by an ambivalence of right and wrong is. His is another long revolutionary tradition of no lesser glory—that of conspiracy. He holds in no esteem the American rebel's emotional imperative to denigrating and insulting enemies. He prefers to attribute dignity and power to foes and their ideological treasure—it gives a better standing to his own protest and sublimates his hatred. He sets the Classic sense of tragedy against the Romantic raptures of his American colleague. While everything that goes on on American campuses and at the peace manifestation trails among skyscrapers revokes the huge Romantic canvases of Delacroix and Géricault—an eventually successful Eastern European upheaval will probably look like Marcus Junius Brutus & Company's famous undertaking.

COMMUNICATION

The American revolutionary struggles against a society that doesn't understand him. Its overwhelmingly vast segment simply has no notion of what he wants. This constitutes an additional reason for the polarization of merciless feelings against *them—their* lack of comprehension and *their* obtuseness legitimates *his* loathing and scorn. The gap widens with every attempt to bridge it. When an American rebel speaks, he rarely does it in his own name; usually he speaks in the name of Vietnamese peasants or ghetto inhabitants, while neither gave him an outright commission of representation—especially the latter, lately known for his reluctance to such proxy. Even the noblest cause, if it doesn't attest to a direct relevance between its spokesman and its beneficiaries, becomes nebulous and triggers countless miscomprehensions, let alone its ability to compress emotions to the revolutionary temperature. The American revolutionary's alienation from his natural planting ground of ideas turns into acerbic disillusionment that consequently transforms into accusation. Being unaware of how gratifying it is to bring those who were unable to grasp at a proper time before the supreme tribunal of history, he thinks himself humiliated but not defeated, which only increases his rage. So he finds himself within a vicious circle where subject, cause, and effect melt down helplessly with object and intention. I often have wondered why this fondly confused interchange of mental stalemates has not yet made the American theater replete with a series of delicious comedies.

The Eastern European speaks, first of all, in his own name. He challenges the existing reality in the name of his personal common sense, conscience, erudition, and set of predilections. Then, without mistake, he relates to a nonenumerated but perceptible segment of his society that anyone, even his adversaries, agrees is present. Nobody ever gave him the mandate to speak in the name of this loosely shaped majority, but the general, all-encompassing consent for his spokesmanship can be distinctly felt, even by the most hostile observers. Anything he says or rather obliquely suggests, is understood in a flash, even by the dullest illiterate. His way of communicating with his countrymen is interlarded with allusions, overtones, subtexts, and innuendos—many of them intricate and opaque, and quite beyond foreigner's grasp—but even the most turgid housewife gets their message perfectly clearly. No anti-Communist proclamation has been ever published, distributed, broadcast, or televised from inside an Eastern European Communist society—as is the case with a megaton of explanatory features and rebel's catechisms in America—and yet everyone knows what it is all about.

The style the American rebel uses to combat his society, the Eastern European uses to fight his society's rulers. The effects are of substantial disparity. If the democratic society shows its ignorance of the rebel's ends, it consequently shows plenty of tolerance and no inclination to serious persecution. The Communist rulers, however, have for their opponents a profound and precise understanding. Therefore they must destroy them.

POWER & INFLUENCE

The American intellectual rebel puts a mark of equation between justice and himself, or his eventual attainment to political power. Having some healthy doubts about the nature of justice—he graciously shuns adjectives like *utopian,* or *objective* in connection with that concept—what he indeed yearns for is power. Unfortunately for him, power is beyond his reach, at least in the foreseeable future. All that is offered to him—at this stage of social revolution in America—is influence; and this seems to him an offensive concession. Hence, he wages a self-destructive war, the hopelessness of which generates a full load of intellectual rabidness and virulence. Being per se more intelligent and articulate than his fellow citizens, he is infinitely more visible in the social panorama. This testifies, in his own eyes at least, to his betterness, and only increases his frustration. Hatred becomes his substitute for power.

The Eastern European rebelling intellectual doesn't miss power. He knows too well what leaden burden is perennially attached to it. All he dreams about is influence. He knows that in enlarging margins of freedom and human dignity, influence is more instrumental than power. The less talkative and visible he stays, the better the chance for gaining influence glimmers in the ever-obfuscated perspective of totalitarian power structure. The paramount of his dreams is the kind of influence his American counterpart rejects with disgust.

DISPUTE

A commitment based on reason and intelligence always endeavors after dispute. It is in eternal search of contention in order to try and probe into one's own articles of faith. An American revolutionary, relying more on feelings than on cerebral premises, adopts an unwilling stance toward intellectual exchange and strife. He prefers emotional fiestas in moods of blooming solidarity and unification with others who feel the same way—a brotherly immersion in the magical community spirit. Some draw a precipitate conclusion by calling into question the intransigence of emotional commitment: the history of political mores in America brings, allegedly, some disheartening examples.

The most striking feature of the antiestablishment movement in Eastern Europe is an unremitting rush to endless dispute. Any quasirevolutionary change in Poland, Hungary, or Czechoslovakia was hitherto preceded by a powerful thrust to discussing by all-engulfing debate. Discussion clubs and forums flourished wherever they were permitted to open. The Eastern European rebel believes in the omni-transforming force of the word and in the almightiness of dialectics. Seemingly not without reason, since each Stalinist counterrevolution used to announce itself first by curbing the free debate, suppressing the clubs, and by insidious, brutal provocations against any form of free-speech gathering.

Discussion was considered by ancient Greeks an indispensable preamble to rational change. This purely theoretical predestination is enough to make it pitilessly banned from any Communist reality. In America, instead, establishment's most blissful reverie is of revolutionary youth discussing issues among the most outrageous profanities, but not enforcing them. Anything can be said, after all, with the blessing of the American Constitution, federal forbearance, and the Ford Foundation. Is it possible that America would be not afraid of rational change without revolution?

LOVE

The denominative value of terms like "revolution" and "revolutionary" falls victim to inflation just as meat and eggs do. Not only has labeling—and self-labeling—recently become a threadbare commonplace, but by dint of a quarter everyone can purchase on Times Square a flaming red button with a rugged inscription, blazoning

in first-person form someone's most intimate persuasion
—until now revealed only at secret meetings or in exceptionally cuddlesome situations. We simply do not
know what to do with words like "dissent," "discord,"
"disaccord," or "disagreement," that have accompanied
men since they sat down around their first bonfire. They
have lost, lately, their hoary usefulness. Literature for
ages had been cluttered with young rebels and iconoclasts
who were wandering defiantly through pages of number-
less masterpieces, declaring their combative devotion to
an imposing gamut of causes. Their abyssmal contempt for the then societal ecology made them poetic
and beguiling; their essential difference from today's
American rebel lies in their well-balanced sense of proportion. They didn't ask love from those they scorned,
wished to eradicate, or, at least, subdue. They hated and
wanted to be hated with no sophistry about love—digging
from their hatred marvellous raw material for their emo-
tionalities that blossomed so beautifully in their verse
and prose. Now, the young American revolutionary hates,
apparently with genuine force, the so-called American
system or way, but, strangely enough, requires love for
himself from all those who love the system and way.
The fully natural and comprehensible lack of love he
calls oppression, forgetful that—save a tiny troop of
early and medieval Christians who indulged in such
transactions—the entire history of civilization has no
marketplaces where love was offered in exchange for
hate. Only very clear, elaborate, and simple visions of
hope or a better life, comprising answers for any question from a simpleton and philosopher as well, had and
have an ability to engender love in human hearts. The
Christian revolutionary in ancient Rome offered redemption and salvation of soul to every wretched of the earth,
by this token generating love that subsisted for twenty

centuries. The Marxian revolutionary of half a century ago offered a new, punctiliously described socioeconomic promise to the exploited and the poor—and was by them loved. What an American revolutionary of today has to offer—apart from rock music, a readiness to instant violence, and grafitti puns—remains opaque. Small wonder that he is generally met with an expanded lack of love and without extraordinary repulsion, called by semanticists indifference. This may also be enlightening on why the movement, in spite of all its intensity, has not created any noteworthy literature nor art, nor anything that could mobilize popular imagination.

Energetic social emotions are, thus, a must to promote a revolutionary situation that would play into the hands of rebels. It would be too much to say that an Eastern European revolutionary is wrapped in a warm blanket of nationwide tenderness. But being respected by his compatriots, he is, first of all, powerfully hated by his ruling autocracy, which he finds not only justified, but much desired. He knows that his modest demands for logic and tolerance represent a lethal menace to their rule, hence their attitude makes sense. It endows him with superb flexibility and gives him an advantage of showing himself utterly negotiable. He can strive just for moderation and compromise and exult in any miniscule gain. He understands that the slightest concession to his postulates is his magnificent victory that shakes the very foundation of the system. And *they* know it too. They try to conceal their adamant will to destroy him behind the trickeries of propaganda and double-talk, but the rebel is watchful. He has to gauge even the process of slackening his ruler's grip of his throat, because a too hasty yielding could rouse suspicions of abuse, manipulation, selling out. There exists a saying in Eastern European political lingo which has a terrorizing meaning for both sides: "To serve one's enemy in an objective way."

MIRACLES OF BALANCE

Once in a while, an Eastern European revolutionary faces tanks in the streets of his cities.

Once in a while, an American revolutionary faces think-tanks in publications and on TV panels.

They are both in an equally dismal position. Tanks are formidable obstacles on the road to a successful revolution. Until the use of tanks is less common than errand boys' bicycles, we can't expect any dawn of freedom over there.

The American rebel, being, in fact, a bundle of kinetic sentiments with a scant amount of intellectual asset to top them, appears to be analogously helpless before think-tanks. We can, however, approach the circumstance from a more optimistic angle. Brutal force, as it is universally known, never prevailed upon the human spirit, hence the ultimate, although very remote, triumph of the Eastern European freedom fighter seems inevitable. Whereas the American revolutionary, succumbing to intellectual violence, may evidently be winning by losing.

PROFESSIONALISM

Social revolutions were usually carried out by professional revolutionaries with the amateurish support of the just-franchised masses. Danton, Marat, Lenin, and Mao—they all were highly qualified pros. There are professional revolutionaries in America today, but, apparently, they do not consider the situation sufficiently matured to sound the big charge. Their meager number and unwillingness to importunate surfacing foreclose the movement's success. For only purebred amateurism grants sincerity, freshness, and poignancy to revolutions, albeit it impairs its efficiency.

The professional revolutionary is unthinkable in Eastern Europe. His extermination, even if he conceived the most fantastic underground network, would be a child's game. So the Eastern European rebel is a strict and compulsive amateur. He can only hanker after his American confrères' condition whose professional activities are confined to making a decent living on turnover preparatives in word and print.

TAUTOLOGY

Extolling violent revolution, an American rebel slips into tautology. A revolution has to be violent by definition. Insisting upon or relishing the adjective *violent*, brings to attention an eventuality that maybe violence is just about the only element of revolution the American rebel is truly after. Change without violence is one of the most routine features of American life, and appeared so commonplace and trite that of late the thought of trying otherwise has occured to the rebel. Why not taste the violent revolutionary version of the old, familiar American-as-apple-pie phenomenon? As cast against slogans and oaths and that huge unkown maze of an unimaginable *revolutionary* future, it may show itself fascinating and exciting.

An Eastern European revolutionary is appalled by the very notion of violence. He craves change without violence. He is more than sure that violence, once begun, will always turn against him. Settling for talks, sitting down at a conference table with his tormentors and indulging in mutual compromises in order to achieve his supreme goals—freedom and the dignity of logic in social relations—would be most cherished by his pride. Only knowing that *that* will remain a wishful thinking, he unwillingly and occasionally resorts to what his rulers call violence, but which has no chance to be considered other than a timid protest by American standards.

SOCIAL STRATIFICATION

On both sides, the middle-class intelligentsia family proves to be the main source of supply for the revolutionary pool. Their offspring come into the world with a commanding conviction that something has to be subverted. Later on, the young American notices that he can change a lot of things around him; but, in the same breath, he's bugged by a penetrating feeling that whatever he can do is always insufficient and lousy. This makes him cynical and idealistic at the same time, which I duly consider one of the prodigious miracles of American democracy.

A young Eastern European, having taken a closer look at what surrounds him, ascertains that he can do nothing to change it. This makes him a very unassuming trier.

WELTANSCHAUUNG

It often seems as if the *Weltanschauung* of an American rebel has been built upon news-media and paperback erudition. In this respect, it brings to mind the modish, pseudoreligious encroachment on meta-physics called—with a dash of unintentional humor— Scientology. It is a branch of modern meditative activities that claims to encompass all contemporary coordinates of feeling and thinking. Certainly it's curious how the theoretical approach to revolution deteriorated with times. One only has to recall the flawless brilliance of the Encyclopaedists, or the grim but impressive con-sistency of reasoning of the Russian bolsheviks. Com-pared to them, the mass-produced argumentation and information of today's leaders and theoreticians loom half-baked and semivalid. And, of course, it's always easier to embrace a simplified message and get inflamed about things embellished by incertitude and incorrectness than to get emotional on well-tested, boring principles.

The Eastern European revolutionary's *Weltanschauung* is constructed of his experiences and structured on autopsy. His empiricism develops early in life when his mother asks him to go and shop for a loaf of bread. Standing on a long line before getting one, he has a perfect opportunity to switch on brooding which will never go off. His inferences are drawn from his condition and well confirm Karl Marx's most favorite tenet: Existence shapes consciousness.

ROCK MUSIC

On both sides, the position of rock 'n' roll music presents difficulties for the strict evaluation of its nature. The Communists think it is imperialistic music. The U.S. revolutionary gurus swear by its anti-imperialistic message. The American establishment makes a tremendous amount of money out of a music that is flamboyantly against it. The Communists don't care for money, but being concerned with their public image, cautiously serve it as a gratification for robbed freedom, thus trying to manifest with its help their fake tolerance and perversely monitored coexistence with the West. Consequently, rock 'n' roll there turns into a bribe and assumes a role legitimately detested by any decent American revolutionary.

JOKE

In Eastern Europe jokes are a powerful weapon and a means of communication as well. They are all about Communists. The funnier they are, the more devastating effect they have.

The American revolutionary commits a grave mistake

by replacing the joke with insult. He thinks an obscenity is a better choice. He tends to overlook the fact that cartoons about him multiply and even the harmless cause him damage.

FREUD

Believing in one's own guilt creates a rebel in America. Perceiving other people's guilt forms a rebel in Eastern Europe. It would be captivating to find out who psychoanalysts would diagnose as healthy.

THE JOYS OF BEING TOGETHER

An unshaken sense of free community, within boundaries of which all decent human predispositions, inclinations, and affections can be honored and practiced, makes the grace, warmth, and joy of the American revolutionary youth movement. There is a feeling of exuberance and openness around it, which endows it with an air of uninterrupted fiesta among meadows where human virtues are gaily cultivated. Wonderous sensations of participation, mirth, and solidarity wrap one up when among the young. Victory signs exchanged at each step between strangers on New York streets, in its parks, boutiques, and luncheonettes, taste like a pretty girl's kiss during *14 Juillet* in Paris, or while attending an Orthodox Easter mass. Having, deceptively, the appearance of a veteran revolutionary, I can tell something about the V-greeting and its flashing up.

Such an atmosphere can be created only in a reality where a free rebel challenges a free society and everyone feels free enough to complain of the lack of freedom or perpetrate reciprocal offenses in a free way. So, consequently, free repressions follow free acts of free confrontation. The only freedom taken away from both sides is that of unlawful persecution.

The Eastern European rebel is devoid of all these joys and satisfactions. Where there is no freedom, complaining of its absence is severely forbidden. He is an enslaved rebel, and faces a sad, gloomy, enslaved environment where every alikeness, commonness, and adherence to the same cause must be carefully checked and fathomed. Most of all he fears provocation.

BLISSFUL IGNORANCE

Each self-respecting XX-century totalitarianism was founded on the concentration-camp principle. There is no evidence, after all, that what the American revolutionary muddily figures to himself as future can survive and contrive without camps—although he is the last one who would have them in mind. But the larger the country, the harder it is to revolutionize it without thoroughly tried-out devices, so much appreciated during turnovers elsewhere. It's rather dubious that a victorious revolution in California would squander possibilities Alaska has to offer.

The Russian rebel lives with the notion of Siberia constantly in his mind. In a country where all but each family has had a member in a concentration camp, it's impossible to stop thinking of it. For an American, camps are not a burning issue. It would be a waste of time to argue, that according to prior experiences, he, as an individual with moral and cerebral sensitivities, would be accounted as one of the first customers of the institution, once it's established by his triumphant leaders. For an America watcher it's a sort of weird pastime to imagine the entire *New York Review of Books* editorial staff squatting in front of a barrack, in a Yukon landscape, and melancholically recalling Coke, hamburgers, Ultra Brite, Radio City Music Hall, and the right to bail.

ECONOMICS

The cry for real *change* is most indistinct in the field of economics. Only the American black revolutionary has a coherent want to change his people's economic condition. His white companion, though, goes through a period of palpable prosperity—usually he enjoys a secured income from his parents and an inundating supply of free pleasures that were economically stipulated erstwhile. He may crusade against the poverty in some remote parts of the country, but he can hardly announce a fight for bettering his own condition. It looks like the times when Madame Sans-Gene laundered the Paris revolutionaries' underwear for free and Trotsky had just a herring with one onion for dinner are irrevocably over. It comes about that a revolutionary leaves a subversive meeting in a Porsche or a vintage MG; the working class, to the contrary, drives GMs, and therefore is accused of *petit bourgois* leanings. Sitting on the dirty floor of a Greyhound station, romantically tucked up in his old poncho, the revolutionary embodies not destitution but stylization—quite imaginative and appealing, incidentally. The blueprint of his revolution contains a few clues of what new economic reality he wants to bring to the liberated masses. All the same, it's hard to detect from them whether he intends to relinquish his present condition, uphold it, or, maybe, improve it. But how? An answer on how to get a poncho and a Porsche without liabilities from his father's business has not been yet delivered.

The Eastern European's economic worries begin, first of all, with himself. An effort to make ends meet overshadows his revolutionary fervor, sometimes corrupts it. Fighting a system that pretends to have abolished economic privileges and being unable to afford oranges for his sick child, he feels himself trapped. What's the alternative—if programatically he is against any restoration of capitalism?

FATHERS & SONS

In Communism, fathers are responsible for the politics of their sons. When sons get arrested during demonstrations, fathers are fired from their state-controlled jobs and deprived of citizen rights.

In America, fathers, under the stress of their sons' argumentation often start taking parts in demonstrations. Mothers introduce themselves at parties: "I'm the mother of a revolutionary."

SHADES OF DISSENT

There are innumerable shades of rebellion, resistance, and dissent in this country. It fills one with awe for the organic strength and abundance of a civilization that produces so many visions of life and emanates so much hope for the future. An American rebel, of no matter what coloring, thus has to combat so many and such disparate sets of values that his task appears inexecutable to everyone except himself.

There is only one single color that is combatted in Eastern Europe. It makes the political scene look drab and morose. No difference who is exhorting whom in what name—nationalism, liberalism, or religion—the issues and slogans are tediously the same: Bread and Freedom.

MORTAL DANGER AND PRICELESS HELP

The American revolutionary's most formidable foe is not the System, nor the Establishment, nor Imperialism. It is another human being's Mind. The pubescence and adolescence of every revolution are simple, idyllic, and come out of sickly doubts. Reason, argument, rationalization, justification, concept, and emotion are then measurable, homogeneous, and solid. What's bad is Bad, beautiful—Beautiful, right—Right, wrong—Wrong. Everything is well ranged and transparent. Here we have the Righteous, and that's Us: There stands the Oppressor, Exploiter, and Boring Parent—and that's They. But—forth comes what Tolstoy mentioned in *War and Peace* as the awakening of intelligence in Pierre Bezukhov who, all of a sudden had noticed the amazingly infinite diversity of human opinion and the enigmatic circumstance that the very same thing can be viewed in diametrically opposite ways by different minds. The superb univocality evaporates after a while, annihilated by the routine burgeoning of contradictions, and the young American revolutionary finds himself in a situation where the Righteous stands against the Righteous, learning thereby the bitterness of factionalism. It's nothing new from the standpoint of history, of course, but rebels make history not learn it. So happens the loss of an idealistic virginity, the world looks a bit different afterwards and everyone has to decide what to do with his own Gnosticism.

For an Eastern European rebel, the aforementioned ability of human mind is a priceless ally. Each spark of man's doubt flipped at the crushing Communist uniformity is a molecule of triumph. They are not scared of division and dispersion, these only facilitate their bills of indictment. The monolithic, blatant, sanctified Communist contempt for human intelligence makes factional fights among them impracticable.

THE TRANSMUTATION OF SPECIES

The young American rebel's social provenience is mostly from the middle class—a social group that defeated a horrible economic depression and won a formidable war against Fascism. Less visibly, but not less firmly and successfully, that group rejected any totalitarian encroachment on its mind, rights, and persuasions. It has never let itself be talked into a so-called collective conscience, which seems to me quite an achievement in times when the treacherous charms of collective responsibilities gave the easiest absolution to many troubles of conscience. Its sons and daughters accuse it today of not having materialized absolute ideals, the common projection of which many of its members had been struggling for quite gallantly, experiencing both the joys of fighting and bitter taste of disappointment.

The young Eastern European rebel's genealogy is more surprising. Overwhelmingly, he is an offspring of the Communist intelligentsia family, and, in many cases, direct heir to great Communist names in politics, culture, and administration. His parents, as a rule, were ardent rebels in their prerevolutionary societies and led lives full of sacrifices. They believed fanatically in and fought stubbornly for the final Communist victory, ideological supremacy, and political power, limitlessly devoting their hearts and intellects to the cause. They organized manifestations bursting with placards, from which we could have recovered plenty of the slogans so popular today at revolutionary meetings in Chicago, Berkeley, and Central Park; they went on trials and sat in prisons. Thirty years later, their sons and daughters accuse them of having perversely betrayed the anticapitalist ideals they proclaimed and still proclaim— only with the help of brutal repression and censorship against all those who dare question and object to their proclamations. Now they stage trials and throw into prisons their own sons and daughters who only want what their American peers so intensely castigate their own elders for. Words come to memory written by someone extremely benevolent to the Communist revolution on the occasion of its fiftieth anniversary: ". . . its quite a paradox that peoples under the Communist rule, as their most urgent need, see an unremitting endeavor after those elementary liberties that were commonplace in all bourgeois liberal programs which we Marxists used to expose to our valid and relentless criticism."

DIFFICULT WISDOM

A perceptive lady has reminded me of an old German saying that in politics, as in love, *es kommt nichts Besseres nach.** I pondered it gravely during my next morning shave, and then I said to myself with relief: "That depends . . ."

* "Nothing better comes after."

8.

On Permissiveness and Correctitude

WHAT'S NEW IN OUR LIVES?

An ad in a major university campus paper founded A.D. 1877:

> King's–Lion RX Center, Inc.
> The Only Discount Drug Store On Campus!
> Save Up To 50% On:
> —Prescriptions
> —School Supplies
> —Birth Control Pills

ROUTINE

Every fifty years, the adult part of mankind feels and maintains that the world has gone crazy. Everything in society, arts, morals, and manners seems to be upside down. Our well-established common sense of distance, time, and shame runs into incomprehensible difficulties and requires a sudden adjustment. Of course those responsible for the turmoil and devastation learn, after a while, that loneliness, envy, the bitterness of unfulfilled dreams, and the eternally unanswered question: "What did we do wrong?" have not disappeared. However, they do not have enough time for meditation. Then comes their turn to complain of the world gone mad.

CIVILIZATION

Among other things, civilization means a convention according to which we humans agree not to burden each other with our too excessive humanity. A wall, in spite of its frequent misuse, remains one of civilization's basic inventions; we have as much need of being separated as we need to be together. The idea of a private bathroom and a shower curtain is as fundamental as the notions of law and community, and as rudimentary as language is a communication medium. A vague sense of what is unbecoming or what one is *not* supposed to do shows itself over and over again a powerful ethical lever, though even Plato was already unable to explain how it really works. Its principle is indefinable. It is also a most delicate instrument, as a matter of fact, and easy to destroy, but no one knows what to replace it with. Neither is it known how civilization would have looked without it. Both the optimism of scientists and the gloom of moralists appear irrelevant.

CULTURE

Paradise and man's natural condition must have been delightful circumstances, but they had nothing in common with culture. Culture begins with the fig leaf. One can say that culture, as a whole, is a nuisance, and many did (the most charming among them, Anatole France), but no one can claim to advance culture by removing the fig leaf. By doing so, he indeed degrades it, albeit the peculiar hypocrisy inherent in culture makes it quite difficult to brand as objective *regress* what might be presented as subjective achievement. Poetry, culture's loveliest flower, seems unimaginable without a *clad* human being. The proudest goal of literature is to deal with the invisible—not in terms of uncovering what is covered, but in order to penetrate the depth and complexity of coexisting forms and attires. An undressed *homo* offers no hunting ground for discoveries. Only the infinite diversity of clothes can give him the value of a bottomless riddle. An undressed woman might be beautiful, but a half-dressed one is interesting—and interest is a legitimate notion from the realm of culture, whereas beauty bears the flaws of naturalness. Art, from its very beginning familiar with the naked body, saw in it primarily a form. Anytime when they wanted to immerse themselves in the meaning and substance of life, artists resorted to draperies, or put hats on their models. Nakedness remained for them, through the ages, a means of perfecting their craft that held them inside the magic circle of culture. And this approach seems to me very wise.

NEOEGOTISM

Egotism—an obtrusive and excessive reference to and emphasis upon oneself and one's importance—had always held a prominent place in letters. European Romanticism owed it many distinguished achievements. Romantic and post-Romantic egotism initiated genuine research into the depths of the ego, which today has passed into the hands of doctors. Many outstanding men of the pen, from Stendhal (who even wrote a *Diary Of An Egotist*), to Proust and Joyce, cruising on much vaster and deeper intellectual waters than the human self, used egotism as a handy vehicle to penetrate the unexplored area of consciousness. Fashionable countenances of *Weltschmerz* and spleen were superbly instrumental in expressing the then up-to-date egotist's disgust with his environment or with the world as a whole. Above all, egotism served as a Geiger-counter of sensitivities, and sensitivity remained the Grand Notion of Western literature for two centuries. And the most delicate psychophilosophical device of human sensitivity was a feeling of shame.

After psychoanalysis deprived mankind of guilt, a thorough pulverization and dissolution of psycholiterary contents began. Goethe, Benjamin Constant, Shelley, Turgenev, and Conrad could still converge on the belief that shame is a virtue and a key to important human values. The last fifty years of literary progress have established shamelessness as a criterion of sincerity. The result is a peculiar brand of neoegotism in today's novel, movie, or theatre, that is obtrusively prone to fingering psychointellectual hemorrhoids or burrowing among the emotional complexities of *fecalisme*. Ingmar Bergman is by all means a truly creative moviemaker, one of the most influential molders of our cinematic consciousness, although, no matter how deeply he reaches into his characters' neoegotistic torments, the audience's response remains deadly perfunctory. "Oh," sighs a blasé film consumer, well-expertised in problems of faulty complexions, "poor man (or woman, or child) . . . ," and forgets the protagonist's agonies five minutes after leaving the movie house. Whereas the much less refined problems of Jean Valjean, Anna Karenina, and Mowglie still bring tears to many eyes and last in one's lifelong memory.

VOYEURISM

Many are inclined to define the contemporary rise of sexual permissiveness as voyeurism. If this is correct, its sources are obscure. The partisans of uncontrolled nudity in public maintain that their ends and interests are aesthetic, for they believe that "the body is a beautiful thing." The more artistic happenings and experimental ballets they stage so as to "help liberate the emotions" or "conquer the audience's fear of the human body," the more obvious it becomes that not the body but certain parts of it have interest for the defenders. The Greeks, the incontestable and legitimate discoverers and true-born connoisseurs of the beauty of the human body, were manifest antivoyeurists. A visit to any museum will quickly demonstrate how little they thought private parts an embellishment. And we have to assume that it was not prudery that inhibited them and induced them to belittle what today's reformers find a new and extraordinary tool of psychical liberation. The sage candor of the ancient Greeks in such matters is well reflected in their history and writings. We must assume then that it was rather a lack of interest that shaped their unsurpassed sculpture.

ON DISMAL END POINTS

When everyone finds it possible to undress anywhere, the individual, private act of undressing loses its intimate and ultimate significance. By advocating its publicness, the staunch spokesmen of individual deliverance through nakedness abolish its individuality and shift it into the category of collective experience. This could prove lethal for so many values that its consequences might transgress the narrow margin of the issue of mores.

Nakedness is the source of most painful inequalities. Clothing is historically one of mankind's most democratic and egalitarian tendencies. Apostles of "spiritual reward through stripping" argue that, once the basic inhibition is overcome and "something is unlocked within," the inequalities and the feeling of shamefulness turn into a benign sense of fulfillment and freedom that lets us forget about them. They just overlook one trifle; namely, that the inequalities do not disappear because one forgets them. The moment they return to one's mind, an ugly sensation follows. One of the highest priestesses of the recent cult of nudity from California proudly declared: "The human body is just another costume." I would say yes; but the only one that can not be altered at any price. I want to believe that the priestess was unaware of all the ruthlessness and cruelty her words conveyed. The atrocious idealistic epistemology of Bishop Berkeley hovering over today's Berkeley campus turns out to be the most irresolvable equation of our time.

BARE-BOTTOM TERROR

A couple of actors, performing in a play with profound ambitions, strip onstage, enter a well-exposed bed, and realistically imitate (let's hope) lovemaking.

It doesn't excite us any more. It doesn't shock us either. It doesn't liberate anything in us, although theatre critics and social commentators claim it does.

What I experience is a feeling of loss. I feel sorry for my depleted sensitivity. I think with deep concern about where my desensitization will lead and end. I worry about what would be indispensable to shock me again. I am disgusted by the theft of my privilege of being shocked. I'm afraid that other people think the same way, but pretend to laugh and enjoy it all under the terror of the false liability of being unconventional, enlightened, liberated, affranchised, and emancipated. But from what?

EUROPE & AMERICA

Is the American kind of permissiveness in morals and manners more licentious, thus more socially harmful and culturally repulsive, than the current European one?

I think it is.

Europe is old, experienced, insidious, and skeptical. Its sense of ambivalence is well poised and, after centuries of refined, sociocultural chiseling, serves now more as a restraint than as a factor in deterioration. It underwent many periods of permissive decadence that never succeeded in completely shattering the radical bonds between eroticism and culture. Woman's position within the European civilization was always heliocentric and much more independent and influential than would be generally acknowledged. This was achieved chiefly because of the tactical finesse of European women, distilled through ages of merciless strife, which favored scoring real gains *without* propagandizing them. Europe is passionless. Its system of mutual correlations between mores and abuse, love and sex, emotion and its sensual implementation has been thoroughly examined and well classified. The most complicated issues were so long researched, tested, and translated into solid and comfortable patterns that a powerful sexual tradition resulted whose abundance of moral and emotional compartments and drawers enables everyone to find his own, warm refuge from any destructive torment, or, if necessary, to find an appeasing solution among the impregnable fortifications of reason, empiricism, and venerable hypocrisy. Many aspects of European life are now yielding to the relentless necessities, blessings and freaks of modern mass society and to its civilizational consequences, but sexual culture is one of the last bastions of unbending Europeanism, in spite of some fallacious signs of capitulation. Sweden's lethargic and schizophrenic asexuality, advertising itself as debauchery, and Spain's volcanic and skillfully tamed prurience, self-adored as chastity, are both European characteristics, notwithstanding any discrepancy.

America's traditional tolerance of crime and felony has resulted in deadening the social awareness to many initial features of the current wave of permissiveness. The American susceptibility to answer appeals to its civic virtues doesn't pair, unfortunately, with its power to recognize evils-to-come. The banal principle of action and reaction has played then a crucial, if rather truistic, role.

Too much was forbidden for too long in America, and the mere fact that today too much is permitted stands in obvious rapport with it. Both prohibition and overexaggerated permission lead to losses; both deprive the sexual life of the same qualities: depth, sophistication, and variety. In 1953, a movie was banned because the word "virgin" was pronounced onscreen. In 1967, a successful New York theatre director considered total nudity on stage "a potent and liberating device . . . we're bound to see more of it." Asked if nudity would eventually reach the point of cliché, he answered with silly self-assurance: "Of course." It's doubtful whether he would have been able to reflect and come up with a reply to the question why we should turn into a cliché and give up one of the most precious playthings mankind has ever gotten from its own destiny, namely, the distinction between intimacy and openness.

For two centuries, a majority of Americans were held in the strict persuasion that sex may serve only to produce children, or sin, or bawdy entertainment. Some forty years ago, Freud, canned in pocketbooks and circumscribed for instant use, began teaching them that sex also produces endless, but not-too-easily-explained, troubles and complications whose sole advantage is of being much *en vogue*. No longer than a decade ago, the bemused Americans discovered *en masse* that sex is simply a part of the eternal *condition humaine* like everything else, grief and anguish included. That it may encompass casualness and tragedy, mischievous grotesquerie and tawdry distaste, random little dramas and lifelong goals, unattainable solutions, inexpressible agonies, impenetrable mysteries, and nondescript perfection. Engulfing this newly acquired sensitivity in a chaotic, bad-smelling tide of permissiveness might prove to be the American crime of the century.

Another of the same breed of New York stage meteorites, who are too inept to think out an idea to its logical consequences, said: "In time people may get immune to nudes onstage." But why? Why must we become *immune* to something that should remain in our lives as a warm, marvelous gift of human existence? Life is no cornucopia of *such* gifts. Why should we willfully transform the splendors of exceptionality into the drabness of the commonplace and affirm it as mankind's grand victory? The same compleat thinker proclaimed: "Nothing done onstage in the context of art can result in immorality . . . ," but he failed to explain who's going to determine what art is, and why his own concept of theatre art, as expressed above, may appear to some as pure imbecility.

I have nothing against those glossy, offensive sex magazines for the quarter-intelligentsia; I think they fulfill a positive social function until they insist on calling their puerile dialectics philosophy. "I'm working toward a better, healthier, saner society . . . ," a well-known New York publisher of titillating tawdriness said in a press interview; and with such statements, we reach a point where the hoary, corrosive European intelligence proves to be a better moral breakwater against permissiveness and stupidity than the American sociomoral robustness. In Europe, sex magazines and smut publishers, if they want to survive, have to operate with an indispensable *clin d'oeil* and a sturdy, cynical assessment of their own moral value. In America, they consider themselves in all seriousness as missionaries because commercial success and social impunity give them the certitude of being approved by Providence.

COITO ERGO SUM

"*You have to get to the point* where people aren't shocked any more," said someone who called himself an underground editor, and was a lead singer with one of the more scatological New York rock groups. "It's not being jaded—it's when people know sex is not a *threat to them*, and they accept it."

I felt a sort of affection for the man. Poor, eternal American Boy Scout, lost among haunting specters of his inherited past. His desperate obscenities, shouted with the help of electric amplification, are his self-defense against his own puritanical idealism that he dreads and can't get rid of. He wants to come to the assistance of and rescue all those whose teeth are chattering in the spooky forest of sex organs. In his utterly-frightened, paralyzed child's mind, forlorn in the unknown, there isn't even a glimmering of the fact that sex might *not* be a threat, that it is a human, not satanic, attribute, and that it has no need of being exorcised.

THE UN-MODISH WORD: FUTURE

Actually, the real *problem* of the permissive society and its civilization is not the present but the future. What is one supposed to do with his life in all those years ahead, if now when one is twenty he has acquired the experience of a hoary debauchee? The amount of experience in the domain of matter given to us by God, nature, or biochemistry, is limited and integral, and the great art of contriving one's life well was for centuries held in the highest esteem. The European literature of the last five hundred years provides countless testimony to the complexity of the issue. In this field, euphemisms are of no help, even if used with the utmost intellectual sophistication and stylishness as an ultimate shield against manhandled good sense. An old, thoroughly tested term "orgy" doesn't lose its semantic and syndromic characteristics, nor its psychological qualification and consequences just because it's called a "love-in." This kind of activity, if exercised in the later stages of life, bears some melancholic charm. Espoused in earlier life, it will result later in some really appalling effects theoretically impossible to discuss and explain. No one ever believes in them before a personal and individual checking.

A hostile attitude toward the objectively-existing world makes sense when someone is of age and can offer coherent reasons for it—which is not that difficult after forty. If someone then resorts to drugs, it's sad but not the sort of thing to arouse any feeling of loss in an observer. If an adolescent starts gibbering about moving inward into self-awareness, an uneasy sensation of helplessness looms in our conscience. We know that no mind-expanding drug will help him to escape from the *trouble* with *existing*, that no one is allowed to leave the *real* world and its perennial, sometimes boring, drama in any other way than by death. An old rake, disgusted with life, has always a legitimate recourse to metaphysics. A young, inexperienced believer is ignorant of that refined trick; instead, he accepts a shoddy gimmick. No matter how far or deep he would move inwardly and deny reality, the outward world doesn't cease to exist. The more precipitate his flight, the more objectively existing reality will reassert itself and turn against the one who tries to turn away from it. A famous Polish postwar novel closes with a scene in which a soldier bends over the body of someone he had shot dead a while ago. "Why did you try to run away, man . . . ," moans the soldier in helpless grief. I'm always haunted by the grim relevance of these words when it comes to the drug problem, and all the irresponsible efforts to turn it into a cultural phenomenon.

A Victory

At some universities, male students are permitted to visit girls' dormitories anytime, free of restrictions.

Young people consider this a major victory of naturalness over prudery, hypocrisy, and bigotry. They do not know what they are losing by winning. Where anything goes, nothing really means anything; everything becomes cheap and uniform. How many subtle and differentiated joys will disappear when the last barriers are torn down. In a few years from now, I'm afraid it will be impossible to communicate their values to people so brainwashed by permissiveness that the impulses that once created literature and the theatre have become atrophied.

GENERALIZATIONS' WISDOM

Freud's theory, utterly generalized, says that whatever we do, we do it because of the sexual impulse. There were other theories before Freud, ascribing the notion of culture as a whole to the same instinct. One of my friends, a French stevedore, maintained that whatever we have done since the dawn of mankind was done in the service of sex, seduction, and carnal possessiveness. According to him, men wash, shave, and compete exclusively because of the existence of women, the latter's activity on earth being solely devoted and confined to response. There is a grain of truth in this, as in every generalization. American cultural output of the Sixties confirms it with the zeal of a neophyte.

SIMPLIFYING HISTORY

Permissiveness is by no means the invention or monopoly of our age. The Italian Renaissance and French Rococo had a licentious record that would be hard to beat. People then far exceeded in refinement our clumsily prefabricated set of pleasures. They also knew how to chisel their depravity into imperishable works of art, which is not exactly the forte of our era. Their permissive hypocrisy and perfidy activated an amoral and literary

sophistication, next to which our bluntness, called by ourselves honest sincerity, appears boorish, tedious, and arid.
The stunts performed by teenagers from the houses of
Borgia, Sforza, and Medici would plant a deep inferiority
complex in our most daredevil Acapulco or Chelsea swing-
ers. The inventiveness, taste, and dialectical skills of the
eighteenth-century French erotic theoreticians would
plunge the spiritual leaders of the American sexual revolution into embittered frustration.

It's also difficult to prove that permissiveness is an
unequivocal mark of decay and decline. Both the Renaissance and the Enlightenment were periods of bloom, and
their permissive societies were extraordinarily strong in
every respect. The reference to the French Revolution as
one of the natural consequences of the permissive Enlightenment may be misleading in many respects, since
the overthrow of feudalism was more the work of the
bulging, dynamic force of expansion than the result of
nihilism, satiety, and self-destruction.

The essential difference between permissiveness then
and now is mainly quantitative. Our permissive model is
industrial, collective, and mass-produced. It has been as-
certained beyond any doubt that the Western mass-society
produces everything in surplus, which in many cases is
the primary source of many of our moral confusions.
During the Depression, excesses of food used to be destroyed so as to uphold the price level; it was outrageous
to see huge stocks of coffee burning when people were
dying of hunger. Since that time, our know-how in producing has increased astronomically, but so has our
mechanism of distribution improved substantially, match-
ing at least our frightening facility for creating material
goods. The blow came from an unexpected direction:
our mass output of goods ceased to be exclusively material,
thus engendering a multitude of hopelessly tangled diffi-

culties, resulting in a sociomoral mess. Among others, we facilitate a mass access to the so-called pleasures of life, the effects of which are still magmatic, and it's difficult to say anything about the new moral codification that may follow. And, according to Karl Marx, as quantity turns into a new quality, all these factors create a new circumstance.

Through the centuries lovemaking aspired to an art. It was considered elite and aristocratic, if not in its nature, then surely in its quest for substance. It was a pleasure only for the wealthy. It was a celestial treat only for the refined. It was a debauchery only for the sophisticated. The populace just made children or indulged in animalistic instincts. Occasionally, rustic lovemaking became as fashionable as peasant dishes. Moreover, permissiveness preserved as a common trait of the upper classes, always managed to perpetuate its own high standards and never slipped into insipid casualness. The "haves" always knew how to maintain a certain infrastructure of functional hypocrisy that was constantly busy eliminating cheapness and the commonplace from what should have been a perennial festivity of the singular and the exquisite. The bed always served as a function of something else—of morality among Christians, of a vital force during the Renaissance, of the cult of sensualism among the rationalists of the neoclassical era, of high-strung feelings among the Romantics, and finally of social snobbery and life career during the bourgeois nineteenth century. Intellect, finesse, taste, sacrifice, courage conditioned lovemaking and elevated it to the level of the art of life. Power, money, or feelings were major devices in attaining it. But such devices had to be acquired. This took time, filled up one's life, increased each price and made every achievement valuable.

The first effect of the output distributed as mass pleasure was the transformation of lovemaking into amusement—accessible, harmless, and inexpensive. What an average well-to-do bourgeois family can bestow today upon its offspring surpasses in many respects what Alexander Borgia could give to Caesar and Lucrezia in order to facilitate their participation in life's glamors. What the rich and the powerful once indulged in in their lavish carriages—the perennial symbols of their social and existential status—everyone is doing today in a medium-sized automobile. The mass-produced bed is a supplement to everyday life—cheap, convenient, banal, and relatively interesting. It doesn't influence human destiny, and it settles nothing. No one is interested in saving souls in exchange for abstaining from jumping into bed; no one exaggerates its place in life. Being in bed has, for the most part, no results at all. With the liberation and total emancipation of women, hypocrisy has been completely defeated, suppressed, and evicted. We fought down bigotry, abolished nearly all forms of verbal and visual censorship, and permitted extreme openness. We no longer have any hypocrisy in our manners and habits, although we are aware of some kind of meaninglessness whose origin no one knows anything about, though it has sneaked in and is very distinctly around. Lovemaking became candid, natural, universal, simple in the noblest sense, and easy in the best sense, though we feel that some unnamed but powerful human reason for such activity has somehow evaporated from human existence, leaving a strange sensation of emptiness behind.

FORM AND CONTENT

Permissiveness is rarely an effect of an individual bad will or of a bad impulse. Rather it is produced by what many consider sincerity and directness, and they attribute moral and social value to them. It is, however, where it's at when irresponsibility and thoughtlessness become indiscernible from moral advancement and intellectual progress. We won't have to wait too long to know how sexual permissiveness annihilates the very tissue of human relations. Sexual interdependence is initially form, not content, but it has the unique ability to transmute itself into a complex, emotional content. Devaluation of form means, in the long run, the destruction of content. Judging by appearances, the shallowness and perfunctoriness of approach affects the form. In fact, it destroys the core and the sense of human togetherness.

MORALISTS

It's curious that our epoch has not bred any Savonarolas or Knoxes. Although sin is a nonword for so many, there is enough to preach against, and enough ominously distorted truths to inflame the most imaginative and talented indignation. But perhaps there is also an inherent recognition of the futility of any effort that causes the silence of moralists. Strictly speaking, what can a preacher do against the assembly line?

PORNOGRAPHY

Pornography is vanishing from our world image. It's time to reflect upon whether this is good or not. The mass production of sexual "sincerity" or obscene "innocence" kills pornography. This may involve a cultural loss. The role of pornography was interconnected with the complex and ambivalent aesthetics of prohibition in the Judeo-Christian heritage. In its classic function of inducing all kinds of malaises of forbidden delights, pornography enriched the sensitivity. Its absence will result in boredom and indifference in the face of everything that should have stayed eternally fascinating.

ON CINEMATIC ORGASM

The notion that everything looks better on the screen is well known to all film students since the movies were acknowledged as an art. Anything it touches, the film embellishes in the most treacherous way. To bewildered mankind the movies have gradually uncovered the previously unknown nature of a bloody brawl, murder, and ideal love. The last few generations have acquired, thanks to the movies, a priceless knowledge about how antiseptic, spotless, impeccable, attractive, glamorous, nice, and easy these components of life can be. Turning its cameras to more up-to-date gustos, the film industry has concentrated lately on the portrayal of sexual satisfaction. "Poor women," commented a lady whose subtle connoisseurship I have learned to respect, "first lies were told about how they love, now they are told about how they are loved."

Fashion's Gehenna

Radicalism in feminine fashion consists of cruelty and brutal offense against other women. Its success endows a part of female community with advantages whose real value is based on the other part's humiliation and merciless deprivation of life's tiniest pleasures. In the end, it proves to be ruthlessly antifeminine. When mini- and micro-skirts imposed themselves as the emblems of triumphant femininity, only well-legged women could feel victorious. Those with flaws in the lower part of their personality were terribly handicapped. Right now, they await their passionate chronicler who will sublimate their recent anguish and daily Golgotha in poetry and prose.

The Glory and Squalor of the Movement

This can also be called: Hippiana, or the poisoned delights of permissiveness and irresponsibility. Or: the inexpressible depths of a preposterous splendor. Or: the sheer pleasure of dealing with the youthful mind confined to its beatifications.

Some consider it a closed chapter. Some see in it an

excess of distorted neoromanticism. I think it is the current American defense of otherness and the bizarre. In spite of the Puritan, and, later, utilitarianist conformism, the cult of otherness—some call it pluralism—has always been frantically defended as the hard core of American ideology. The same goes for the bizzare or the expression of a higher ranking independence than the ordinary freedom of expression.

It is also the best top proof of unsurpassed American wealth, and the best indication of the robust health of the American socioeconomic system. France could afford *La Boheme* when it was the most affluent nation on the Continent; so too England and the turn-of-the-century dandyism. But these were minor sociocultural phenomena with no statistical impact, next to which the hippie movement, affecting several layers of social texture, appears like a massive factor. Large numbers of people all around the country who openly declare that they want to live but not make a living, and consider any productive work as "selling out," nevertheless have to eat, sleep and perform other functions without offering anything to the common effort save their colorfulness. The coquettish cheapness of the attire, disdain for goods, modesty of demands, self-elected poverty, and lack of needs do not reduce the global tab. One of the movement's heroes epitomized the problem in a superb allocution, perpetuated later as a widely publicized ad for his records. "You take this electrical power out of the wall, and you send it through the guitar, and you bend it and shape it and make it into something, like songs for people, and that power is a wonderful thing," he said. But he doesn't bother with the insignificant, sleazy, not-worth-mentioning detail that someone has *to produce* that electrical power that he takes so metaphysically out of the wall. Or that without that long line of countless producers, the corporate ones and the "sell outs," his guitar would be dwarfed to its factual dimensions, losing its ability to be instrumental in the technological enhancement of an antitechnological movement. In the present-day world, only the marvel of American socioeconomic sophistication can afford the ultimate luxury of idleness on such a large scale.

It seems to me that the movement's meanest disservice to its own generation consists of the successful replacement of manhood with boyishness in the current hierarchy of customary values. If the female psychological and moral status underwent some interesting transmutation, adding to the girl's image a new depth, torment, and maturity, the hippie male is generally a loser, acquiring traits that in the long run can have only stultifying effects. The corny boyish records voice a boyish self-adulation and exhibitionism, and an ardent, unshaken belief in the imaginary values of boyishness with a sugarlike arrogance that so easily turns into a suspicious squeak. Immaturity is placed on a pedestal once reserved for the set of qualities that enabled mankind to survive in times of crisis. The unacceptable idea that a boy should become a man is repudiated with an obsessive fanaticism. An impressive arsenal of arguments, from infantile exorcism to ridiculous political accusations, is brought into play whenever the occasion arises. They *want to* remain boys perennially —overwise and ignorant, sentimental and cruel, extravagantly joyful and unexpectedly hysterical, with no responsibilities, plenty of pimples, and the unabridged right to sloppiness flaunted as a manifestation of spiritual independence. Of course, they have also elaborated an ebullient code of dogmatic values, but they are incapable of its dialectical defense—a very boyish trait. A deep concern arouses the failure of the status of fists among them. The fist, its mystique and its use, was always the great Ark of the Covenant between a boy and a man. Along with the priority of an eunuchoidally colored voice goes a predilection for the knife—a nasty boy's pet toy. An American writer recently praised their valiance and bravery in fighting the police during student disorders and riots. He seemed to forget that boys are always adventurously courageous in the anticipation only of minor injuries; they seek relatively painless evidence of their bold spirit of challenge. The writer called them heroic, somehow forgetting that heroism is inevitably associated with eschatology. We've got to see the same boys when faced with the eventuality of ultimate payment before we judge their audacity.

Whether they gain the symbolic designation of "children of the century" remains still indefinite, although it is their dearest ambition beyond any doubt. Their juggling with words and notions is occasionally charming but dangerously and repulsively irresponsible. Love and happiness are strange vocables—too often and too insistently repeated, they lose their magic and even sense; too obtrusively introduced, they arouse suspicions and turn into the most mawkish of all insincerities. We have yet to learn how many lives have been broken because of the irrepressible use of words among them. With all the rational reprehension I feel against them, I have for them also an unlimited weakness. Their unwashed, shaggy image with the world's cleanest and most imposing architecture in the background seems to me the hopelessly bemuddled epitome of the tenderness of our age.

And if of late we see less and less of them on the streets, and their big-city communities exhibit distinct features of deterioration, degeneracy, and pathetic decline, we should be aware of the simple and sad fact that the movement is already in the hospitals. The time of payment for the Day-Glo days came sooner than anyone who's twenty years old expected.

LOVE

The generation in revolt seems to associate the basic word "love" with various meanings that correlate with quite different lexical exponents. Humanness, charity, compassion, clemency, loyalty, sympathy, comprehension, mutual understanding, human solidarity, communication, and a natural penchant toward other beings are well-fixed notions, thoroughly explored semantically. Moreover, they have a more precise significance, better tested in language, history, literature, and human behavior, than has love, the exact knowledge of which eludes us—we only know *how* it reveals itself and acts. Seven thousand years of poetry and music has tried to register and codify its manifestations and revelations; but until now, we are still far from a complete understanding and even further from the exhaustion of its unpredictable eventualities. One thing that seems to be fairly well researched, however, is the influence of permissiveness on love, both in the social atmosphere as well as in the individual rendition.

One of Christianity's greatest discoveries was a modest observation that the sinner longs more intensely after the ideal good than the nonsinner does. The more one sins, the more one covets innocence, but, at the same time, the innocence is ever further divorced from him. This subtle formula applies smoothly to our torments with love—the more one abuses love, the more one craves love and the less one is able to feel and obtain it. Whenever we equate or identify sex with love, the same holds true; by detaching sex from its strictly personal goals and endowing it with quasi-social tasks, the permissive society brings it down to a drab, ordinary, though by no means new, set of deficiencies. Sexuality in itself may be a magnificent component of life; but the more it is an all-pervading factor, the less it has meaning. Hence, in order to sustain sex as a "delightful adventure" or a "miraculous herb of life," it has to be protected from devaluation and it deserves the creation of a special psychomoral sheath that would preserve its splendid victories.

Lest we become stranded with sexual life equated with nutrition, we have to safeguard its exceptionality. By refusing to accept nudity in public as a proof of progress and emancipation, we act as if we are preserving the sense of intimate exclusivity of a naked body for exceptional moments in our lives. This is the very marrow of the human right to something *more* than simple vegetation. It has complicated ontological ramifications. In an epoch when God has been declared dead, the absence of sin is obvious *per se*. However, the yearning after the bare existence of the notion of sin must be deeply rooted in human souls. The feverish preoccupation with guilt in modern literature proves it better than anything else. All possible forms of guilt are exhaustively exposed and examined in the contemporary novel, theatre, and movies —save one; that is guilt for one's own life caused by the uncontrolled, amorphous permissiveness of one's environment. Nonetheless, we should know where the euphoria of the up-to-date liberated, free-wheeling woman ends and where her anguish and grief begin. We should know what price she pays for the annihilation of the intensity of feelings by permissive mores—one of the priceless attributes of woman's maturity through the centuries. "Women are as free to be predatory as men are," a silly clergyman said, as if in a caricature of a response, during a silly discussion sponsored by a silly sex magazine, "and we have to adjust to that." "One of the things *we're* discovering is that woman is not sexually passive," added another spirited clerical theorist-become-expert, apparently unaware until now of what the Babylonians knew as well as any liberated East Village smut peddler, and of what he could have easily learned from the Bible. Sad though it may be, anyone who is submissive to permissiveness has nothing new to say on the subject.

THE OUT SIN OF COMPASSION

What to do with one's life when everything has been tried by the age of twenty? Oh, something will always be found; life knows no vacuum; it regenerates itself. Besides, the ideologues of permissiveness do not care for such a detail as *one's* life; they prefer to remain noble purveyors of the slickest principle and fearless defenders of the facile. The almighty American news media, so heavily responsible for the current *laissez-faire* in mores, have little interest in the above question either, except for more newsworthy suicide cases. A national magazine of a serious social impact features a story about *groupies*, an *in* but not original behavioral phenomenon consisting of girlish-feminine sexual aggression against the juvenile rock musicians *en vogue*, and haphazard lovemaking at any price and in every possible way, reminiscent of the weird madness of scalp-hunters. The magazine likens such proceedings to "the women who gravitated to the nineteenth-century British Romantic poets," gleefully forgetting that these women were after individuals, and their alleged contemporary equivalents are after whole groups, often composed of a dozen males, but this may be a typical omission for which the mass coordinate of our time might be blamed. The magazine quotes a former "groupie" who says: "I'm thirty-three, and I've made it with all the early biggies and more. You know what I've got to show for it? Three kids from three different guys—which three, I'm not sure. I've gone the dope route, been busted twice, and taken the cure at Lexington, Kentucky."

The most staggering comment is: "*Most* groupies may be luckier." So writes the magazine that claims the title of moderate liberalism, thoughtfulness, and immense influence in this society. Above all, in its editorial enunciations, it pretends to the highest merit of enlightened responsibility. Yet it shuns the word "some" instead of "most," as if ignoring the fact that the overwhelming majority ends with viewing its past like the girl quoted, and as if closing its eyes to the dismal fact that a frightening number of other girls will be pushed onto the same path by that small, insignificant word "most." This I call the depersonalized impudence of the American press.

On Deficiency

"*Tradition?*" *a young man repeated* after I used the word. "What do you have in mind? What does *it* mean?"

I didn't feel like explaining. As a matter of fact, I didn't know how to. It seemed to me impossible. At the same time, I saw clearly how much petty, loathsome disgust fills the days, nights, emotions, reflections, and deeds of all those who try, or have tried, to live without any tradition. Tradition is a vengeful and intricate value. The denial of its existence strikes those who deny it with a perfidious accuracy. Consciously, or not, everyone, whether an individual, a group, or a community, strives to establish a tradition. The efforts of its persecutors to defy this banal truth exposes only their ignorance of themselves.

The Sources

With no gross error, we can trace the modern permissive trends back to the fashionable attitudes in cultural criticism. By the beginning of the century, the incoming hegemony of psychology in contemporary civilization started the long-lasting disintegration of critical criteria. The moral argument deteriorated to the role of an often-ridiculed convention. The most sophisticated attempts to restore its value, such as those of Kafka and Camus, were successfully countered by the churlishness of political pseudomorality and the growing influence of psychological relativism, which frequently perverted literary ideologies and imbued them with hysterical and masochistic subtexts.

As the effect of such a literary and critical hierarchy of ultimate ends, we live today in a permissive dissolution of anything but an explanatory criterion. Literature and art, under the pressure of all-pervading permissive criticism, have almost renounced their didactic value, both direct and parabolic as well, limiting their goals to a more and more sterile research of the human ego, its bad odors, grotesque deformations, and futile contortions. A situation has been created in which any allegiance to basic ethical norms, or the attempt to make a critical assessment by means of timeless values, is chided by the critics as infantilism, simplism, or second-rate literature, theatre, movie, and so on. The perennial, glorious tradition of posing moral questions, both a sacred privilege as well as a sacred duty of literature since its dawnings, has been abandoned of late for the sake of a pretended effort at listing aberrations, considered as literature's new glory by contemporary critics. Thereby, the critics have institutionalized a unique paradise for operators with shrewd, dirty minds. Erudition has become the only norm for a critic, casuistic reporting eliminating in his work any valid evaluation. Certainly, the critics' degradation has turned against them. They have lost the sensitivity for perception that once gave them the creative status of the great eighteenth- and nineteenth-century critics. They have appeared lamentably helpless in the face of countless fakeries. The majority of works they are wont to praise with a characteristic lack of reticence, and award prizes to, usually sink into oblivion within months after critics' initial avalanches of superlatives. The critics avenge their defeats by manufacturing more fake values out of doleful mediocrities, which stultifies them and subsequently increases their rage and frustration—and so we enter a *perpetuum mobile* of herd instincts presented as sophistication, boredom acclaimed as depth, barrenness offered as finesse, and cynical smartness introduced as thoroughgoing objectivity. There is no exit from this magic circle, for the slightest attempt to defend the simplest human decency would endanger the critics' position in a permissive society they helped to shape. And this is something the critics can afford least of all.

SLIMY HEALTH

The bus passes by a moviehouse featuring a flick notorious for its obscene bluntness. One of two boys about 14 years old, sitting across from me, says: "Have you seen it?"

"Yes," the second answers. "Nothing special."

And he shrugs his shoulders with a convincing lack of involvement.

The boy doesn't know it yet, but he is already crippled. Neither his parents know it, nor his older brother, nor his sister who took him to see the movie, since admission is hypocritically "prohibited" to minors unaccompanied by adults. Something has been left out of his life that he is unaware of but will miss later. If he doesn't brag in vain, and if he really has seen the movie, I would prefer his referring to it with an excited squint in his eyes, muttering: "Man, believe me, I could tell you . . ." The apostles of permissiveness would certainly call such a gaze morbid.

GLOOMY PROSPECTS

The vengeance of literary "honesty," "openness," and "bitter end innocence" upon literature itself will be terrifying. It will take almost everything and leave almost nothing from literature's substance. The everydayness of sex is just the beginning.

A Heartening Eventuality

The opening lines of an autobiographical novel, written and published some twenty-five years from now:

"My father, that debased user of marijuana, whom I had to contend with since the very beginning of my precocious fight for clarity and cleanness against his lowbrow subjugation to all kinds of mystical muddle and litter, constantly tried to repress me and coerce me into the bedlam of liberated instincts. There was always money for LSD from the corner dope-pusher, but never for milk for me and my little sister Gladys. Our drab household was cluttered with horrible canvases of ugly, pornographic conformity. My poor mother was restlessly forced to endure his utterly primitive lack of jealousy and the obnoxious, repulsive, petty, lower-class demand for her unlimited emancipation which he extorted from her tantalized ego with an incomparable brutality. . . ."

What Next?

This question we hear around more and more.

Nudity in front of an audience is like relinquishing the last remnant of an eventuality. After stripping, nothing is left in terms of further communication. The subsequent act, in order to expand the sphere of the *si nommé* artistic discovery, and the realm of the *si nommé* cognitive penetration, can only be copulation onstage. Or socking the person in the first row in the nose. Let's assume that we have already reached these peaks of libertine culture, then—what next? Because there must be something next, since we all believe, more or less, in the idea of relentless progress.

The ideologues of nudity in public assert that the naked

cast can still discuss Schopenhauer or sing arias. I doubt it. It would be like trying to write a poem on a piece of wood with a quill-pen. The perennial essence and raw material of philosophy and art have always been, and still are, the multivocality and ambivalence of depth, not the obviousness of the surface.

Sweet Sincerity

A *middle-aged gentleman*, whose delicate sense of life's alleviating disparities I came to admire, said: "Half of my life I've been a swinger. Anything hip in outlook and idea at once captivated my alacritous adherence. My courage in defense of, and my militant apostlehood for, the new, nonconformist impulses were directly proportional to my limitless devotion and unshaken faith in my righteousness. Besides, it was an excellent time to be different and against norms, and *for* all the extraordinary things that are so hard to accept. I had a constant feeling of delectable superiority, of that ineffable sweetness of ruining without harming, of extorting recognition coupled with smiles. Now I feel bored with that attitude. Everyone feels so affranchised and independent that the emancipation of instincts, penchants, and predilections begins to taste like very cheap food that one has to swallow because he has neither money nor time for anything better, or is too dull and dumb to innovate something else that's fresh. I begin to dream about the simple delights of being a square—a staunch square by choice, who is intellectually conscious of his virtues and takes solemn, well-justified pride in his beliefs. A person who gives a new, glorious sense to that mistreated, abused, tortured, slandered, but so fascinating word—*convention*. I begin to perceive the perverse delectation of temperance, and of faithfulness in love, and I catch myself being transported at the sight of an unobtrusive but prepossessing necktie."

HEROISM

In the very center of New Orleans' Vieux Carré, in the womb of the city's bohemian–artistic neighborhood, we find a restaurant—one of those exquisite New Orleans' restaurants—where we read on the wall:

"La Cuisine de la Bourgeoisie."

It's not a discreetly located decoration but a proudly exhibited announcement over the cash register. By the same token, this inn is more than a restaurant; it is a highly spirited institute for the preservation of values. In an era of universal contempt and hatred for anything *bourgeois*, it displays an ideological courage that seems admirable. I think it more heroic than a topless cellist.

CORRECTITUDE

These days, correctitude is the only nonconformity. Courageous is the man who is sufficiently heroic to be legitimate.

CONVENTIONALISM

Noisy pseudo-antiopportunists in an age when a blow-up is considered art claim that conventionalism equals cowardice. The opposite is true. Permissiveness is today's opportunism and conformity. The alternative to conventionalism is a tepid, shallow, boring chaos of indifference, dull oppression of rudimentary necessities, poltroonery in the face of any decision originating from a definite and detectable value. We have arrived at a point where struggle represents for a conventionalist only choice, and conflict involves audacity of solutions. We are heading toward a reality in which the richness and the pride of existence will be determined by loyalty to conventions within which we will look desperately for charm, beauty, and the way to get the most out of life.

A Perspective Illusion

Today, as a hundred years ago, young people dream about eternal love and happy marriages. When they divorce, five years later, it's our epoch that they hold responsible. They contend that neither marriage nor eternal love are possible in our time. They do not know that marriage was always quite an impossible enterprise or at least perversely difficult. And love was never very durable, to say nothing of eternal. Thousands of years ago, humans knew that as well as we know it now, though they have been maintaining that, by sticking to so-called principles, one can manage both the inconveniences of marriage as well as the troubles of love. This proved to be the source of many memorable dramas and well-known stories; but, conversely to our contemporary beliefs, it somehow worked out. Whereas today we have ample theoretical preparation on how to deal with the respective worries, and even ampler freedom in avoiding every damaging inhibition or constraint. The all-pervading discontent remains, however—a most characteristic feature of our time in this domain.

A Premonition

After the youthful inversion of values and the current reevaluation of emotions, the simple feeling of jealousy will be the first to make a triumphal comeback. The next generation's literature will rediscover its poisoned thrills and tyrannical agonies of self-defeat.

The Underground

Everyone who lived through World War II on the European continent knows that the underground denoted the armed resistance movement against the Nazi invaders. It is a sacrosanct word in many countries until the present. It was, and has remained, a synonym for heroic clandestine activity, endangered by lethal issues at each step, a symbol of the relentless fight against the overwhelming forces of Fascist oppression. A member of the underground had to be prepared to pay with his life for his participation. Anyone who survived will never forget the sacrifice of those who fell.

In America the word "underground" is currently used by persons involved in producing and selling erotic literature, photographs, and movies. Their activity is fully legal, undergoes no persecution at all, and somewhat enjoys commercial popularity. Why the producers insist on using this euphemism remains a mystery. They do not cherish any struggle. They do not live even in accordance with advertised and propagandized values. They do not have enough guts to back the proclaimed slogans with practice. They dwell in their comfortable suburban homes, surrounded by families, meticulously avoiding any bout with vice, leading the life of righteous middle-class burghers with a little shady income. One may well describe their position as obnoxious and cynical. It may also be that the word "underground" is one of the Puritan relics of dishonesty and insincerity in the language. But words take revenge. In the moment of need they may turn against tongues that have martyrized them.

THE GLORY OF GENERAL BADEN-POWELL

The American intelligentsia's drive toward obligatory permissiveness bears some aspects inducing one to deep reverie. The boy- and girl-scouting tradition gives a very interesting effect when adapted to the radical pornographic cause. Many of them consider the universal appeal to unrestricted copulation somehow equal to the impulse that, in accordance with the best scouting tradition, commands them to help an old lady to cross the street.

The Happening and the Very Recent Past

Happenings, as performed of late, are a sort of *tableaux vivants*. A striking difference between them and the popular pastime of Louisa May Alcott's epoch is the fact that the little women are now nude. Occasionally, a garbage can is blown up with the help of mild explosives or simply set afire, which symbolizes an act of creation and substitutes for the uninspired chores of painting or sculpting. The artists and directors of staged "love-ins," or other happenings involving nudity, want us to observe a naked human body in an emotionless way, or at least in a way devoid of the regular human emotions that used to accompany such a circumstance until now. They claim that depriving ourselves of any excitement, or any other feeling of exceptionality, will create in us a new and more valuable awareness or will even testify to our superior humanness. In their demands they are in harmonious accord with the not-so-outdated proclaimers of an analogous principle. Their predecessors were the SS-men in charge of the Auschwitz crematorium. They, too, looked with an indifferent, cool, and depersonalized eye upon the throngs of naked bodies, depriving them of their usual human significance of nakedness. They scored their artistic achievement of the parallel elimination of human feelings some twenty-five years ago, and, I presume, the American and French *liberated* artists of today may feel a little flat at being so upstaged. Leafing through an American quarterly devoted to the most advanced ideas in theater, not long ago, I ran across some pictures of happenings packed with nude men and women. The periodical considered them, naturally, of paramount theatrical accomplishment. I had a strange sense of familiarity. The Nazi-sponsored newsreels and pictures of the Oven Era came so oddly to mind.

THE MYSTERIES OF THE DEFEATED IMPULSE.

Anything that pertains to emotion can be pretended on stage. The talent to pretending we call acting, and it has a superb tradition that goes back to mankind's dawnings. The better one pretends, the more skillful and talented an actor one proves to be, and the more success one scores.

Anything that pertains to the mastery of physical impulse and response we call acrobatics or circus art, and it, too, has a glorious tradition in human civilization. It was, and it is, publicly performed, admired, and respected as the control of the body; and an ability to obtain a maximal effort from it always was, and is, in highest human esteem.

Of late, a singular new quality of showmanship is hailed and presented as an unique skill and sociocultural liberating force. If observed more closely, it makes an impression of insensitivity or downright numbness. It consists in taming the sexual response, and is extolled as a service to human progress in the field of humanness itself. Individuals of both sexes perform on stage gestures and acts which involve the most sensitive parts of their personalities with no normal reactions that, since millenia, have been recognized as regular for human behavior and grace. This is called an achievement by theater critics and social commentators. I would call it mutilation.

THE ECONOMETRICS OF PRODDING

The role of sex in culture is that of a blessed stimulus. This everlasting and sanctified position was recently undermined by the chaos of uncontrolled openness, that distorted the proportion of interchange between *homo* and culture—the most effective purveyor and distributor of stimuli. Many who create in the name of culture have lost their sense of what to create and how to create it, and thus uphold their influence upon man and their sway over stimuli. It probably will lead to the atrophy of cultural stimulus in general. Yet evidences exist that *homo* can't live without stimulus, and when he can't get it from culture he looks for it elsewhere. Mayhem, concentration camps, and cruelty have proved until now to be the best substitutes when culture has gone.

"LA NUIT ET L'INSTANT"

At the nadir of the French Rococo, Crébillon-fils, a libertine writer whose openness would cause the New York *avant-garde* to blush and whose finesse would poison them with a corrosive envy, wrote in his novel *La Nuit et l'Instant*, one of the hallmarks of the world's lewd literature:

"Perhaps we are even unaware of it ourselves, but despite the fact that everything we understand by principle and decency is so much discredited these days, we still feel a need for them . . ."

LEOPOLD TYRMAND

New York
May, 1969